Pirates

Golden Age of Piracy & History
From Beginning to End

(Surprising Story of the Caribbean Pirates and the Man Who Brought Them Down)

Calvin Manning

Published By **Tyson Maxwell**

Calvin Manning

Pirates: Golden Age of Piracy & History From Beginning to End (Surprising Story of the Caribbean Pirates and the Man Who Brought Them Down)

ISBN   978-1-990373-91-6

No part of this guidebook shall be reproduced in any form without permission in writing from the publisher except in the case of brief quotations embodied in critical articles or reviews.

Legal & Disclaimer

Table Of Contents

Chapter 1: Story of Piretes

A number of notorious pirates in time past terrorized the same seven oceans. They were quite different from the friendly pirates depicted on"Pirates of Caribbean," the "Pirates of the Caribbean" film series as well as other films however their actions remain popular today. Some of the world's most famous pirates began their careers in the form of privateers, sailors with state authorization to hire who snatched merchant ships in certain areas and fought the opponents of their countries on the sea. But, the people who were getting petty viewed those hire guns in the same way as pirates. Other people who began with official employment, resorted to piracy after the lure of gold was too tempting, so they embarked under their own flags to rob the wealthy vessels of merchants illegally.

At the peak of colonial expansion, when global trade expanded, lucrative merchandise was transported across oceans, creating multiple opportunities for piracy. The period with the most dramatic drama of sea-based savagery was during the golden age of pirates (c. 1680s - 1726) in which more than 4000 pirates per year were terrorizing the Atlantic as well as the Indian oceans. A large amount of important cargo was transported over vast oceans in the period that was colonial growth. When European navy slowed down, many experienced sailors inactive did go into the world of pirates. In this book, you'll learn about the many pirates that ruled the sea in the golden age of the sea.

William Kidd

William Kidd began his career as a pirate, and then made the decision to employ European monarchs to strike foreign vessels. Kidd was at odds with the British administration when his team refused to stop attack on this Quadegh Merchant the massive Armenian ship loaded with gold located in the Indian Ocean. He was executed in 1701 in London to serve as a warning for the others pirates. The legends of captain Kidd and the honor of being to have buried in the Caribbean are numerous, and he is still one of the most thrilling and fascinating pirates.

The year 1645 was the time William Kidd was born in Dundee, Scotland. Kidd was a man whose father is believed to be a seaman and had been a swimmer when he was a kid. After interacting with a variety of Buccaneer crew members, he was an admired privateer by the 1680s. At the time, Kidd sailed to America to seek a fresh lifestyle and later, wealthier prospects from New York, where he was able to marry a rich widow. As the tensions among England and France became a full-blown conflict, Kidd was tasked with guarding the Blessed William for the purpose of helping protect English vessels in the Caribbean from French attack.

Piracy was an elusive industry in the past. When countries employ mercenaries such as Kidd defend their wealth but it was understood that they could earn the benefits of enemy vessels with their treasures. Kidd was able to learn his trade when he was a young sailor of the age of. Also, it was an era which was drawing to a closing.

Kidd traveled to England in 1695, to attend an inquiry by the parliamentary committee for being pirate. He was there to meet Lord Bellomont who was appointed to the governor's office in New York. Kidd was accepted by Bellomont. He was also provided financial support to sail into the

Indies with a similar team and also strike French as well as pirate vessels. Kidd as well as his comrades and the backers of his would split the loot confiscated. Kidd embarked on the adventure galley with a gun capacity of 34 in the month of May 1696.

Unrest soon took over the company. A number of Kidd's employees died from the disease, and as Kidd was able to locate a few French vessels to strike He was now under greater pressure from exhausted and unhappy crew to keep the journey profitable. Kidd led his crew towards Madagascar around 1697. the destination of many pirates who made their money only on the Indian Ocean. The attacks on several Indian ships led to minor successes. In January 1698, the fortunes of Kidd began to be changing when he saw that the Quedagh Merchant smoothing the tip of India.

Quedagh Merchant Quedagh Merchant was not your ordinary vessel. It was a massive 500-ton Armenian vessel that carried goodsan enormous treasure chest filled with jewelry as well as spices, silk as well as other treasures that was owned by the Indian Minister of the Grand Moghul. Ministers have great contacts. When Kidd's assault was discovered and expressed his displeasure about it to East India, a large and mighty English trading company. Kidd is quickly branded up as a wanted criminal because of the changing perceptions of pirates among a variety of governments. Kidd embarked on a new ship, called the Quedagh Merchant, after abandoning the decrepit Adventure Galley. Then, he made his way to a small ship in Boston which is where he was detained and sent into England.

Kidd was tried on May 8th, 1701. The crimes he committed, along with his previous close ties to the English top officials and the elite caused quite a controversy. In defending him, like Kidd predicted Lord Bellomont and other would be, could only damage his image and reputation. On the 23rd May, 1701, Kidd was found guilty and sentenced to death. The body was hung in a prison and put to rest for all to view.

Black Caesar

Caesar Later, dubbed "Black Caesar," was an pirate in his time in the Golden Age of Piracy. He was a member of the Queen Anne's Vengeance of Edward Teach and was one of the crew's remaining members following the death of the Lieutenant Robert Maynard killed Blackbeard. Legends of his life, including his being African royal and had brutalized his fellow pirates in the Florida Keys for years before the start of Blackbeard were interspersed with stories, legends or fictional stories, as well as others of pirates.

According to the legend, Black Caesar was a well-known African popular war chieftain. He was able to escape various traders of slaves because of the "huge size, enormous strength, and keen intelligence." Caesar was eventually caught by a slave trader who took him and 20 of his troops to a vessel. The trader gave the trader a watch and offered the soldiers and him additional items that were "too heavy and also too innumerable to bring onshore" should they decide to the ship. The trader enticed them to stay by providing food, percussion instruments silk scarves, silk scarfs, as well as jewels. However, the men were ordered to start lifting anchors and then sail off at a steady pace.

As they sailed towards the Florida coastline, an unexpected storm's appearance threatened and destroyed the vessel right at the Florida Reefs. Conscient of the imminent doom for the ship the captain ducked beneath the decks to free Caesar. They then rounded up the crew and captain, probably with a firearm as they climbed aboard one of the longboats to get ammunition and other provisions. The waves crashed and pushed them towards shore, and they seemed to be the sole remaining survivors of the ship that was sunk.

Then they began using the lifeboat to get vessels that were passing by to stop and assist. They would then take boats across the water and pretend to be whaling ships and then offer to bring passengers aboard. As they approached the ship, they would pull out their guns and demanded the materials and ammunition in the hope of sinking them in the event that they were not provided. They continued in this manner for many years, amassing an impressive fortune, which was then buried in Elliott Key. The sailor and he, but, they came to the ground and came across a girl who was who had been resurrected from the vessels they taken from. Caesar was killed by his friend from the past by a fight and captured her.

As time passed as time passed, he fought many pirates, and was prepared to destroy ships in the open ocean. The crew and he frequently were able to avoid capture when they ran into Caesar Creek and other inlets between Elliot or Old Rhodes Key, as and also onto mangrove islands. The rope was braided through a metal ring that was embedded within a rock. They then moved the boat in a heel and covered their vessel until the guard ship, or another danger was cleared. The boat could be lowered by the same mast, and then capsize it in the shallow waters, after which they could remove the rope, or pump the water out in order to raise the boat, and then continue their attack.

Though no treasure was discovered on the island there is a belief that the gang of men left 26 silver bars in the sand to be laid to be laid to rest.

The harem was said to be a part of the cult in his home, and he was accused of capturing around 100 women on vessels at sea, and also the military prison in which the inmates were kept within stone huts, in intention of paying ransom. After he quit the island in raids, he made no rules for his prisoners, and many of them died from the effects of starvation.

Some children are believed to have fled from their captivity eating fruit and shellfish, and forming their own customs and cultures. The lost society of children led to the local notion that the archipelago was plagued by.

Chapter 2: Edward Low

Edward Low is remembered today as one of the most famous pirates from his time during the Golden Age of Piracy. In his time of prosperity in the west, he swarmed the coastline across North America, earning a reputation for being a ruthless pirate. His stories of the brutal punishment of captured vessels and passengers soon became known to the government of America as well as England. They quickly branded Low to be one of the top sought-after criminals of the past and began to organize a combat against the ever-growing pirate fleets throughout both the Atlantic and Indian oceans. A lot of historians debate Low's passing and the contradicting reports of his last months.

Low was born in 1690, in Westminster, London. Being a part of a family with a modest income She quickly slipped into the world of crime. As time passed, the gang was involved in increasing serious crimes before deciding to leave England to try to make it in the modern world. Once he was in America and moving from one city to another until 1714 when He married his bride Eliza Marble, who died shortly following the birth of Low's sole daughter.

His wife's passing brought him back into the gang scene that he was a part of in his younger years. Low, along with his crew members, quickly set up a rebellion against a captain, and seized the ship following a brief stint as dockworkers and fellow crew members. Low currently Captain of a pirate who was able to seize some trade ships in the waters between Boston in addition to New York, allowing him the opportunity to migrate to profitable Caribbean waters. Once he was at the Grand Caymans, he quickly became a lieutenant to the well-known and experienced captain of pirates Captain George Lowther, who shortly granted him the command of his large, six-gun Librantine boat, "Rebecca."

The fame of Low grew steadily through his time as a pirate. He was able to catch 13 fishing vessels moored at the Port Roseway harbour. There, he picked one of the larger fishing vessels to serve as his brand new ship "The Fancy." The majority of his captives were killed in the course of his exploits throughout the Caribbean and tales of his crimes were spread throughout the Atlantic. A lot of victims of his pirate assaults identified Low as a psychopath, who loved taking out his anger on other people; Low often chained, cut and burned or had captives devour their captain's heart.

In 1723 Caribbean officials had had their fill of Low's heinous crimes and ordered a force to eliminate him as fast as they could. In June 10 of 1723 Edward Low's entire fleet was smashed with the help of English captain Peter Solgard and his warship HMS Greyhound. Although the crew of Low's suffered casualties in the fight but he and his skeleton team of A Fancy were able to escape. Low has gotten more brutal toward the vessels he was able to capture in the following year until his group put on a show of force and left his ship in a secluded location. According to some sources the source says that he was spotted by the French who executed him in Martinique when they learned what he had been doing. In other accounts it appears that he was able to escape to the United States and lived out the rest of his days in prison.

Francois L'Ollonais

How often can we say that someone is a celebrity? It could be when somebody rips a person's heart in order to find out more?

Maybe when someone decides to devour a prisoner in order to get more treasure? Jean-David Neu, a Frenchman is well-known for his exploits as a naval officer throughout the Caribbean.

The nickname he was given his name was Francois L'Ollonais, but he was also referred to for his role as "Flail of the Spaniards" for the adversities that he committed against the Spanish citizens. Maybe he has his motivations, but the brutal treatment of his prisoner was unprecedented in the past of pirates. And, perhaps most importantly was that he wasn't even an pirate. Jean-David Nau was certainly one of the cruelest buccaneers in the world.

The year was 1635. He was born in France. He was sold when a young man by the maestro, who eventually took his son on a trip to the Caribbean. He served as a slave in Martinique's island Martinique from

1650 until 1660. On his part acquired confidence and knowledge throughout his later successes in his career. He joined in 1660 the same gang of buccaneers who retreated to Saint-Domingue and showed his skills. In the years that followed until the last day of his existence the main focus was on robbing and taking out Spaniards.

L'Ollonais was appointed captain of a tiny ship by the governor of Tortuga, who was also known as a buccaneer. Nau was brutal, stealing several ships, and killing all who was onboard. L'Ollonais was one of the first buccaneers to organize land invasions.

The ship was destroyed in the Yucatan Peninsula in 1663. All the crew members survived the catastrophe, however, the local Spanish soldiers killed the survivors. The only one who survived was L'Ollonais because of his deceit. He was covered in the blood of deceased friends and acted silent. He dressed himself up as the Spaniard and fled through canoes, accompanied by salves that which he released. When he arrived at the Tortuga An angry Nau destroyed the entire Spanish ship, leaving only his tiny team. One man was left to tell the legislature of Havana of the perpetrators.

The man he was with found a new companion with Michel de Basco, a famous Caribbean sailors. They assembled a massive group of 600 raiders, and eight ships. Cities like Maracaibo and Gibraltar within the Venezuelan Gulf were snatched by the pirates. Fortifications in Maracaibo had 16 cannons that were used to protect the city. L'Ollonais on the other however, deceived the defence by attempting to strike on the side facing land. Fortifications were quickly destroyed and the area was left wide exposed and vulnerable to destruction. The buccaneers landed in

Maracaibo and discovered several citizens left. They chased them in the woods, and finally apprehended their fugitives. In L'Ollonais, they tortured nearly all citizens to betray acquaintances and reveal hidden treasures. Many people were killed because of their torture.

They then arrived at Gibraltar and launched an abrasive assault, which resulted in the majority of their victims. The town was quickly taken in their grasp after the 500 security guards were killed. Residents were slain in the same way similar to those who were killed in Maracaibo. Everyone was subject to the same fate because they were sex-assailable or tortured and then killed. A few of them perished without any apparent motive apart from their personal happiness. Then, in L'Ollonais" rage, all of the town was destroyed. The buccaneers returned to their homes with 260,000 pieces of eight from the pillage, and ransom.

The year 1667 was when L'Ollonais was planning a second massive attack and brought together more than 700 raiders to carry out activities within the Caribbean. They quickly seized Puerto Cabellos' port Puerto Cabellos and had already set out to seize the town of San Pedro. The Spanish invaded L'Ollonais while on his journey to the town and he only managed to escape death. L'Ollonais was furious and seized the meat cleaver, and beat the heart of one the hapless survivors. The other survivors who were terrified revealed the most efficient way towards San Pedro, which was quickly conquered.

Both towns, however, were stricken with poverty There was a plethora of worth of treasure to be found. A lot of discontented buccaneers left L'Ollonais, leaving one boat and a crew. The man believed that this was enough for a victory over Nicaragua. The remaining ship was destroyed in the journey to this town at the beginning of 1668. The pirates decided to take a go across Darien in Gulf of Darien, but they were eventually resued by the Spaniards. When they tried to flee, L'Ollonais was apprehended by Indians who were on his Spanish side. The end of his life was what he might have been due to. He was mangled and burnt. According to legends that he was eaten by cannibals.

Thomas Tew

In the 1690s Thomas Tew was among the most famous Red Sea pirates. In the Royal Warrant granted to Captain Kidd for his hunting of buccaneers in 1690, the King William III specifically mentioned him as an "wicked and ill-disposed person." When he first arrived at Bermuda around 1692 there was a minor identified as Thomas Tew. According to certain reports the man was from a rich family in Rhode Island. In the French conflict, he was employed as a pirate aboard English vessels. Tew was appointed as captain of the ship Amity Endeavor.

Thomas obtained permission from Governor Bermuda to hit French vessels and colonies along the African coast. Tew was scheduled to become a member of in the Royal African Company and attack an French manufacturing facility located in Goori, Gambia, with Captain George Drew. When a storm shattered Captain George Drew's vessel, Tew decided to abandon his plan and turned pirate. The crew quickly enlisted his help to join him because the initial mission was risky and their pay was not enough.

While traveling towards on the way to Red Sea, Tew came upon a large Indian ship that had more than 300 troops and seamen. But, Tew and his raids were able to take on the Indians! Tew won in a short battle and his troops received an amount of PS3,000 to share. Tew chose to battle against the remaining prisoners when he learned that the vessel was a part of a convoy. But the quartermaster as well as all of the crew were not in favor. Tew and his team, decided to choose Madagascar for their next destination.

Tew later went on to Rhode Island and acquired a pardon. The fugitive stayed a few days and then "the lure of a sea and the attraction of the lure of a "grand accounts" were too great to resist." Tew seized a fishing vessel and set sail towards an adventure in the Red Sea. Tew took on a huge vessel belonging to the Great Mogul at the time of 1695. The next time, Tew was well-armed and he suffered fatal wounds in the fight.

Chapter 3: Bartholomew Roberts

Bartholomew Roberts would easily win when all pirates took part with each other in plundering ships. Roberts was perhaps one of the most efficient pirates in history. According to the legend, he purged 400 vessels, and his bravery was the key cause of his longevity. Through all of the Caribbean Sea, this fearless captain threw a wrench into every ship which he encountered. It included many of the most powerful ships, that most pirates prefer not to encounter at all cost. Roberts is also known for his role as Black Bart, which symbolizes his brutal actions. Roberts as with many pirates, didn't decide to join the piracy industry for himself.

Bartholomew Roberts has been characterized as an attractive, tall person who is fond of wearing expensive jewelry and clothing. The actor was often seen sporting the most stunning waistcoat in crimson and an expensive hat that had an attractive feather in red. The man was in good style even during the battle. A large chain of gold with an engraved diamond cross was draped on his chest.

The man was born in Wales and was known by the name of John Roberts. He spent his youth aboard various ships in preparation for his life on sea. He was slaved during his time as the Third Mate aboard the British slave ship called the "Princess." Howell Davis, a pirate took over the ship off the shores of Guinea. The Pirates made Roberts to join the ship's crew. However, John soon realized this business was an ideal opportunity for his.

The young man appeared to be a good young man right from the beginning and soon was Davis his favorite. Davies as well as some of the pirates died during an ambush that occurred in the month of June 1719. In spite of his short time with the crew, the group elected Roberts as the new captain. Roberts was given the title Bartholomew Roberts and started his journey as a pirate. In revenge for Davis's death, through the destruction of the harbor and constructing a pirate ship, the pirates headed towards the coastline of Brazil in search of a place where they assaulted and pillaged several vessels, including battleships. The Portuguese were taken hostage of many merchandise.

The American colonies became an ideal target. In the beginning, he offered to sell all of his haul as well as the pirated ships across New England. In a matter of moments, the Newfoundland harbor was destroyed. More than 20 ships that were captured were burnt by Roberts as well as his pirates. The French ship, with 26 cannons was the only exception and was referred to as"the "Royal Fortune." Black

Bart used that name for his entire fleet of ships throughout his entire career.

Roberts seemed to be an intelligent person. However the other hand, he was an than competent pirate, who didn't hesitate to do apprehensions. He was once caught by the slaver who was carrying around 80 slaves He then burned the vessel which killed the entire slave population that were on the ship. The reason for this was that he did spend little time or effort in freeing those who were suffering.

Roberts brought the entire fleet together to his side as his fame soared. The pirates of the sea began to travel along the American coastline during the summer of 1720. as more ships were seized up to the Caribbean. As the fleet landed in the West Indies, this same terrifying captain unleashed another storm of violence by snatching fifteen English and French vessels. This time, the most prized item was the Dutch navy vessel with 42 cannons. In spite of the bad conditions, the efforts of his to travel to Africa did not succeed and the Pirates had to be forced back in the Caribbean.

The gang was able to pillage additional vessels. They also captured the legislative officer of Martinique and many other. Since the legislator was Roberts enemy, the pirates seized his warship, and hung the politician. A brand new "Royal Fortune" was soon added to the fleet and was the first French warship that had 52 cannons. Finally, they made their way back into Africa in 1721. many survivors were purged across Nigeria as well as Liberia. As his final day neared the Royal Africa Firm's ship "Onslow," was the most important prize to be seized.

The British government sent Captain ChallonerOgle to locate and take down

Roberts at the beginning of February 1722. The warship he was on "Swallow," pursued Roberts out of the Caribbean and pounced on his ship, the "Royal Fortune." The Pirates are in the waters off Cape Lopez, where they were celebrating. The fighting began with Bartholomew Robinson was the first to fall. The man was killed in the midst of battle when he was hit with grapeshot The stunned crew dumped his dead body in the ocean. If he were to die, dying, it was his intention. The pirates were unable to last all that long without a captains, so they gave up shortly afterwards. Captain Ogle was also able to take Roberts smaller ships of his fleet. He also discovered an enormous amount of gold inside the vessels.

Benjamin Hornigold

Benjamin Hornigold is a classic illustration of Benjamin Hornigold, a classic example of a Caribbean pirate who resorted into piracy after the conclusion in the War of the Spanish Succession. He was however, destined to have an additional task in his life however, he was turned into an infamous pirate hunter. Some are describing him as an experienced leader, who dealt with the prisoners with more respect than the other pirates. Hornigold was most likely best known for his relationship with the famous pirate Blackbeard.

Though details regarding the private life of his seem to be a mystery Hornigold was an outstanding commander and leader at that period. After the war was over and there were no jobs available, Hornigold set sail from Staten Island and became a captain of pirates. The captain had a number of skilled pirates in his team Some of them including Samuel Bellamy, went on to be more well-known and prosperous than he was. Naturally, his most well-known pupil was legendary Edward Teach, also known as Blackbeard.

Hornigod was aware of Blackbeard's potential as well as his abilities, and granted him Teach the ship of his choice and a crew of a few as well as the title of captain. The two sailed together with the intention of becoming partners. They effortlessly robbed a number of ships all over the Caribbean Sea and the American continent. They took a valuable French Dutch Flute, "Concorde," which was loaded with 26 guns while on the way to return. It was one of Hornigold's most memorable prayers during his time as a robber, and also his final prayer.

A lot of Caribbean pirates opted to ask forgiveness from the King after their arrival Woodes Rogers who was the Governor of Bahaims. Hornigold was a former pirate. accepted amnesty. He then left Blackbeard and pirates. He went back home to New Providence, and he was a faithful serviceman. This led to the relationship he had with Rogers was amazing as was the governor's opinion. highly of him.

Horingold was the privateer, or more specifically, an armed pirate hunter. His main target was Charles Vane. However, he failed to catch him even though He was the one responsible for the death of a lot of Caribbean pirates. Apart from John Auger, the others were largely unnoticed. Hornigold's journey of trading towards Mexico began to become a murderous affair in 1719. The vessel he had built was destroyed on a reef off coast, and Hornigold and his whole crew perished.

Calico Rackham Jack

Calico Jack was regarded as one of the most famous pirates who ruled across the Caribbean in the Golden Period of Piracy.

He was not a champion fighter, however he didn't made a fortune, however his name is still remembered by contemporary public better than many others who are true legends of pirates.

John "Jack" Rackham did not earn the fortune or respect that pirates earned during their limited time as an Caribbean Robber. In fact, he received the name "Calico Jack," but his ties to pirates around him as well as his own unique pirate who included two female pirates as part of his crew, made him people be one of the most well-known pirates ever. The man was not considered an outstanding fighter, or as a skilled naval strategist. However, his shrewd brain and the ability to utilize global affairs and backstabbing in order to achieve his objectives helped him become one of the most distinctive pirates.

The published works that came out after the death of Calico Jack significantly led to his fame and his eventual rise to the popularized pirate lifestyle led to the mythology of Calico Jack to expand. His Jolly Rogers flag also significantly affected the current image of pirates. The majority of pirate crew members utilized designs depicting humans in skeletons that were wielding weaponry, Calico Jack elevated an famous flag that was illegally downloaded which has come to be associated with pirates of the sea the black flag that featured an unpainted skull of a human in white and two white paws that managed swords that crossed beneath the flag.

The writings that were published after the death of Calico Jack significantly increased his popularity, as did the final popularity in the popularized pirate lifestyle movement helped the legend of Calico Jack to spread. The Calico Jack's Jolly Rogers flag also significantly affected the current image of pirates. Although a significant portion of pirate crew members wore flags that showed fully human skeletons posing with weaponry, Calico Jack elevated an famous flag that was illegally downloaded which has come to be associated with pirates of the sea - an all black flag, that featured a human head in white and two white paws that managed to traverse swords under the flag.

The peak of the influence of Jack Rackham occurred in 1718, when Captain Vane was forced to withdraw when he was confronted by a massive French warship, at least two times as large as The Ranger at the end of a long run by pirates. Vane had a vast experience as a Sea commanding officer at that time and knew that taking on such a huge vessel was not feasible for his tiniest vessel that had been recently subjected to several pirate raids, but was desperately in need of replenishment for repairs.

The group was split because of the retreat and the retreat was a stalemate, with Rackham in charge and criticizing Vane of taking a poor decision. After the meeting, 15 of the group backed Vane's decision to withdraw. In the meantime 75 of them claimed that taking the French ship would provide them with huge sums of money as well as the opportunity to establish a new base which would enable their crews to be pirates aboard one of the largest and most well-equipped ships.

Rackham scheduled a vote for November 24, 1718 and Vane was exiled from the position of captain and labeled as a smuggler. The crew of the Ranger's was quick to elect John "Calico Jack" Rackham as the new captain and Vane and his followers were permitted to depart on a small boat that was carrying ammunition and food.

Calico Jack proceeded with the pirate races after he was promoted to captain. His efforts were targeted at small passenger and merchant transportation vessels. In one of his adventures, he was able to take control of a number of larger ships. However, the largest reward he could ever win was from the holdings of the huge Jamaican vessel Kingston. He took on and seized the ship with confidence and skill, however for him, the fight had a full view of every government official as well as merchants based in Port Royal.

Disappointed by the behavior of the now famous pirate Merchants in the city gathered in a band. They armed with a pirate-hunting Spanish ship, with the aim of capturing and executing the captain Calico Jack. There are some historians who dispute the sequence of events and the end result could result in Captain Jack and his crew were able to escape the pursuit. In the report of Captain Charles Johnson in his book of 1722 "A General Background of the Robberies as well as Murders of its Most Notorious Pyrates," John Rackham managed to escape the Spanish ship, making use of the low tides, which stopped his Spanish warship from advancing towards the anchored in the vicinity of a pirate sloop on to the Cuban coast.

Calico Jack and his crew were able to row two boats towards the small sloop that was recorded by the Spanish which was anchored next to the warship in the night. The pirates smashed through the guards of the ship and fled, leaving the Spanish warship spotting that the pirates were missing early in the morning after which it was not enough time to hunt the pirates.

Different versions of the story provide a variety of events that took place when Spanish chasers pounced on the flagship of Calico Jack Kingston that was located close to at the Isla de Los Pinos off the coast of Cuba. Rackham and a lot of his crew escaped being captured by hiding on the shore and awaiting pirate-hunting ships to depart, taking all their possessions as well as their wealth and treasures, along.

In the wake of this defeat and the loss of his captain, the captain Jack and his crew made the decision to avail the latest amnesty deal offered by the English government (specifically the Governor for the Bahamas, Woodes Rogers) in which pirates would be able to continue living as a free man provided they give their lives to pirates and privatizing. They traveled to Nassau to tell authorities that the captain Charles Vane compelled them all to join the pirate ranks. The governor Woodes Rogers acknowledged one's plea partially because the relevant authorities were directing him to take significant efforts to address the issue of piracy within Caribbean waters, however there was a deep resentment of Charles Vane.

John Rackham, and his pirates, received Royal Pardon, with the condition that they could be executed in the event that they went back to the piracy. The lure of sea was just enough for a lot of them. John Rackham did not stay an upright citizen for very many years.

Rackham was agitated and agitated in Nassau and caused a stir by being involved in an affair with Anne Bonny, wife of the sailor James Bonny, who Governor Rogers Office also employed. When he learned about the affair, James Bonny begged the governor to let his wife go on the flinch and get her married, however John

Rackham intervened, offering the governor money to get her divorced legally. Without a peaceful resolution to be found, Rackham and Anne Bonny took the decision to cancel his Full Pardon through the theft of one of the sloops from the harbor before returning to pirates. In hiding in the pirate crew were Mary Read, some other female pirate who had initially hidden her gender from the pirates who disguised themselves as a male. Captain Jack and his lover, Anne Bonny.

After returning to the sea The captain Calico Jack and his crew started their regular runners against merchants across the Caribbean. Apart from attacking merchants, Calico Jack targeted a handful of tiny pirate vessels to not eliminate competition but rather to give them an possibility of joining his team. Calico Jack created chaos throughout the Caribbean within a mere two months. He commanded the ever-growing pirate force. At the end of 1720 Bahamas governor Woodes Rogers has issued a proclamation that declared Rackham and the entire crew as pirates. Jonathan Barnet, a pirate hunter, took to the water quickly, and set sail for Jamaica and claiming Rackham was able to capture a couple of tiny fishing vessels.

Captain Jonathan Barnet discovered Calico Jack's an anchored sloop in the waters of Bry Harbour Bay in Jamaica during October 1720. After an intense session of plundering, the captain was able to impress pirates who were having a drink and partying. As per reports, the crew members of the pirates were led in the scuffle by just Mary Read and Anne Bonny. The fight, however, ended in a short time, and led to the capture of whole John Rackham crew. Captain Jonathan Barnet took them all to Spanish Town, Jamaica, in which they were tried for the crime of piracy, and were sentenced to die via hanging.

Captain John "Calico Jack" Rackham was executed at Port Royal on November 18 1720. He was executed by lynch, gibbeting as well as hung on an islet that's now near the entry point of Port Royal's harbor in order to provide a cautionary tale to pirates everywhere in the Caribbean. In the book "A General Background of the Robberies and Murders of its Most Notorious Pyrates," Captain Charles Johnson recorded Anne Bonny's famous remark regarding Rackham: "If he would have fought like such a Man, he need never be hang'd like a Dog."

The remainder of his group was executed with the exception of two females named Anne Bonny and Mary Reid They were confined to jail for months, until the claims they made about their pregnancy were confirmed. According to the reports, Mary Read died in prison on April 17, 1721 and the records indicate that Anne Bonny stopped. It is unclear what happened to her today, but certain sources claim that she was released after which she lived an unhurried life at the shore until her passing due to the effects of old age.

Chapter 4: Edward England

His birthplace was in Ireland, in the Republic of Ireland, and Edward Seegar was his name. Edward England's journey into piratery started when he was an enlisted mate aboard the sloop. Captain Winter was a pirate who abducted the ship from Jamaica for transport to Providence. Then, he earned the trust of pirates and has since become among their leaders.

As the majority of his crew resigned to the King in exchange for his pardon. Edward England continued to not accept the offer and was eventually forced to leave his home in the Caribbean. Woodes Rogers, who was the Governor of the Bahamas and former pirate is the person who sacked his fortress. The Irishman was required to travel towards Africa to continue his the robbery.

It was an extremely successful voyage in bringing many ships along with his. "The "Cadogan" was particularly intriguing " Bristol, a vessel led by the captain Skinner. He was in debt and had grudges at England's crew. In the end, his torture was gruesome and he was murdered. In that boat, Edward was also able to meet Howell Davis, who became famous and a popular pirate. Davis was given command on"the "Cadogan" by England because they saw lots of potential within his character.

Captain England began his first swap of flagships later. He swaps his sloop with one of the ships known as the "Pearl." ". The flagship was commissioned and named "Royal James." It was a smart choice even though pirates were comparatively effective in this thriving context.

The pirates came back to Africa during the spring of 1719. They seized several ships in the waters off Cape Corso. Certain were just robbed and then allowed to go and others were later joined to the pirate's fleet, and then burned. In the same period, ships like"Queen's Revenge," or "Queen Anne's Revenge" or the "Flying King" from the pirate fleet was separated from England's flagship ship and sent across the Caribbean. Edward England swapped his flagships again. "Fancy," the "Fancy" took the place of the "Royal James." It was even more formidable Dutch vessel.

Captain England's next harassment was during Madagascar and Madagascar. He had the two most successful "actions" and continued to expand his influence. Pirates attacked two English and Dutch ships on Johanna An island that lies off on the shores of Madagascar in 1720. and also the East Indies Company owned those vessels.

Two ships managed to be able to escape. However the captain James Macrae's "Cassandra" remained to engage the forces of Captain England. In the event that vessels came to a stop and the fighting continued for a long time. Then Captain Macrae is required to run to the shores, leaving his cherished ship. "Fancy "Fancy" was utterly destroyed with pirates suffering many more deaths.

Captain Macrae eventually surrendered to pirates, who planned wait to see him after some days of starvation in the forest. England's first mate John Taylor, planned to behead him and exact his revenge against the "Fancy's" 90 men. However Captain England was not aboard Macrae, so he was aware of his courage and wanted to save his life. Captain Taylor finally agreed to it after a long period of convincing and a few layups of Rum. To make up for it, the pirates opted for their own "Cassandra."

The Captain England's crew in contrast they were not happy with the decision. In the end, they were pirates and the thought of the idea of letting captain Macrae depart was a huge mistake for the crew. A mutiny was declared against England and Macrae was imprisoned on Mauritius alongside the faithful followers of the three Captains. England had the ability to design an oar to travel on a voyage to Saint Augustine's Bay in Madagascar. But, Edward England died as an infirm man within just a couple of years. Maybe he wasn't worthy of the fate he suffered because his generosity was unmatched. pirate to ever.

Howell Davis

Howell Davis was a beautiful pirate who was not dependent on guns and strength as the captains. He took advantage of bribes, disguises, and bribes to get what he wanted due to his intelligence and sharp man. The life of a pirate was short however it was exhilarating. Davis was a lifelong resident of the sea, spending his as a child on vessels. He displayed exceptional talent and experience, which is why the title the chief mate was highly deserved. His career as a pirate began with a sudden halt in the year 1718. Edward England, a well-known Irish pirate, was able to capture this salver-sloop "Carogan," on which Davis worked. Howell amazed by England and his pirates decided exactly what he'd decide to do next, or join the group. Since Edward England lauded Davis' capabilities, he was immediately the captain of pirates. Davis received the command as a "Carogan" because compassion was one of the primary traits of Irishmen.

He dropped the anchor to Brazil. The pirates were expected to market their "Carogan" here anyway, however, the crew was awed by the vessel and persuaded the captain to reconsider his decision. Instead, they took off towards Barbados for the purpose of unloading their cargo. Davis was accused of piracy in Barbados and was imprisoned for about a month. Davis was released however since there was no evidence to support his case. Davis's next destination was Caribbean Sea and the Bahamas islands. Woodes Rogers, head of government in the Bahamas had to make Davis modify his plan. Davis was on board Rogers the sloop "Buck" and persuaded the crew to rebel. Davis was, naturally, was appointed as an interim captain at the time the incident occurred.

Davis and his team seized the two French merchant vessels on the waters of Hispaniola. The second vessel was equipped, however they were deceived and swiftly caught. Captain Davis would like to change that ship to become an pirate vessel. They erected a flag of pirates on the ship, and forced the prisoners to surrender their weapons in order to act as pirates. With no shots fired the unsuspecting opponent surrendered. He was able to conceal his technique. This was an uncommon skill to master this art. Davis was a superb actor, as well as a Bluffer. He often tried to be a seller or a pirate hunter, to trick unsuspecting enemies. His charismatic skills earned him respect and appreciation from the group.

Davis's actions later on occurred along his West African coast. At the time, another important pirate was also a part of his. Bartholomew Roberts was the name

(Black Bart). He was a third-mate on a slave vessel that pirates took. In the time before his death the man was Davis's most sought-after and favored apprentice. Davis was once dressed in a man's attire and went to the Royal Africa Company Fort. Davis fooled the governor of the town to invite him to dinner. Governor Davis was arrested, and raped for a huge amount of money. Numerous vessels, including a large Dutch boat, got plundering during the following period. The most valuable, however it is "Saint James," a battleship with 26 guns that astonished the pirates. In the end, that vessel became Davis his new flagship.

Paulsgrove Williams

Paulsgrave Wilson, born in 1678 was born in Rhode Island. He continued the family's tradition of becoming goldsmith. He met in 1715 Samuel Bellamy, a poor sailing sailor, who had traveled to the Caribbean seeking lost Spanish treasures. Williams was so enthralled by his new companion that he disbanded his family and children to pursue the dreams of his friend. He also helped to pay for Samuel's second treasure hunt.

In the midst of searching for the treasure that was buried, Paulsgrave William along with Samuel Bellamy decided to become pirates and make a fortune no matter what. Bellamy was the pirate so that he could make a fortune quick and then return to be an admired captain. But it's not clear what made a man of 38 who was already wealthy and had a wife, children and had a lucrative career would choose to be the pirate.

Paulsgrave Williams was an extremely accomplished pirate. He was a captain on Bellamy's ships. was the quartermaster, and also the second in command. Samuel handed over his ship the "Mary Anne" to

Williams after they captured the ship. In just a few months the gang robbed more than fifty vessels. Williams went off by himself after Bellamy's tragic death in the month of April 1717. But, with his companion gone his piracy, it was not so appealing for Williams. He resigned the next year in peace.

Stede Bonnet

Stede Bonnet was an major in the army and also the proprietor of a plantation located in Barbados. Bonnet is often referred to as an "pirate gentleman" due to his ethnic background as a pirate, was among the most interesting and unique pirates of Caribbean time. Although he was not the most efficient, Bonnet became famous due to a number of his non-pirate actions.

Bonnet left the army and resided with his wife on a huge land close to Bridgetown,

Barbados. The lucrative sugar plantation provided the owner wealth as well as a pleasant and serene living style. The year was 1717 when this man of middle age with no reason began to engage in the world of piracy. According to legends, Bonnet had a lot of arguments with his wife and was dissatisfied with the daily routine.

Stede Bonnet had only been on the water for a couple of days on the sea, and had little about pirate life. So, in contrast to every other pirate Stede Bonnet was able to purchase his vessel! The Sloop "Revenge" had ten cannons. It also had around 70 competent crew members from towns around and began his "adventure" across the Caribbean Sea. As a weak navigator and leader with no experience the strategy of needing to make sure they were paid well was a good strategy in order to avoid being removed. But, Bonnet was able to take and plunder some smaller vessels near the shores from Virginia along with the Carolinas with the help of his experienced team.

He was not experienced in the ocean and didn't have any experience with pirates' life styles. Stede Bonnet therefore purchased his own ship, not like the other pirates! It had ten cannons and was a sloop named "Revenge." He began the "adventure" across the Caribbean Sea with the help of 70 competent seamen from close cities. He escaped being ejected for being a poor seaman and was a fresh leader with a plan to reward them with a generous salary. But, Bonnet was able to take and plunder some smaller vessels from the coasts in Virginia along with the Carolinas in large part due to his skilled crew.

After the famous siege of Charles Town in South Carolina that he observed from afar

Bonnet followed Teach's suggestion and headed straight to Bathe Town, North Carolina in the hope that governor Eden, the "pirate-friendly" governor Eden would give him amnesty. Since he was likely to back be captain, Bonnet decided it was best for him to join his privateer forces during the conflict in the war with Spain.

Bonnet However, he was tricked. Blackbeard had went away Bonnet along with his "Revenge" and 25 pirates on an isolated island after seizing all his riches. Bonnet returned to the command in"the "Revenge." In the conflict in the conflict between England and France and the French, he left for his home in the Virgin Islands. Although he was not able at times to chase Blackbeard and his new-found status, the privateer was determined to take revenge against him.

The majority of Caribbean criminals who were pardoned usually didn't have legal jobs but instead continued the crime of stealing ships. The same is true for Bonnet. In a short time, he changed his name for his boat in to "Royal James" and resumed pirate activities. With more knowledge, Bonnet could easily plunder several ships along his Virginia coast. The pirate robbed a ship in the local area as he was repairing the ship at the outpost for shipping in North Carolina, and the announcement was made to the same officials within Charles Town. It wasn't just him to have caused trouble in the area in the Caribbean; Charles Vane was an additional. In order to find pirates, the authorities in the area hired William Rhett, a ship owner in the area.

A group of hunters discovered a pirate lying within the Cape Fear River in October 1718. Then, they targeted Bonnet's flagship. After Bonnet was ordered to surrender following a battle lasting five hours as he pursued Charles Vane, Rhett was surprised to find that Bonnet was aboard the vessel. As the pirates entered Charles Town, locals recalled the fact that Bonnet was a part of Blackbeard's team for production in the famous attack.

Prior to his trial, Bonnet was detained at the privacy of a residence. There, he sent a letter to a governor, asking for forgiveness. Bonnet tried to escape however he failed. In 1718, Stede Bonnet as well as thirty other pirates were executed through hanging for their involvement in the piracy business.

Chapter 5: Emanuel Wynn

French pirate Emanuel Wynn, also known as Emmanuel Wynne, Emanuel Wynne as well as Emmanuel Wynn, operated in the 17th century. There is little information about Wynn aside from the fact the fact that he played a role during the 17th century and in the Province of Carolina and later was involved in a battle against Spanish and English vessels operating within the Caribbean.

British Admiralty Record, the sole source of information written regarding Wynn is the only source of information on captain John Cranby of the HMS Poole ship was engaged by Emanuels the pirate vessel near the Cape Verde Islands. Wynn successfully escaped the pursuit of Captain Cranby near the same island of Brava, perhaps with the assistance from Portuguese soldiers.

Perhaps the first robber who was able who flew the Jolly Roger was Emanuel Wynn. His flag has the crossbones design that is the most popular pirate symbol however it also has an hourglass symbolizing that the pirate's target has ran out of fuel. The other explanation behind the theme of an hourglass can be explained as the one method by which for the predator to escape death is to walk before it is too late. Although he is not a very popular pirate, different versions of his flags are often seen in the contemporary tales of pirates, for instance, 1980's films Cutthroat Island as Well as the animated One Piece.

Peter Easton

Apart from being among the most famous pirates of the nation of America, Peter Easton was an Englishman who was regarded as one of the top pirates ever. His birth date was around 1570 in the period between 1611 and 1614 in which he was plundering, came to the notice of officials for being a sea pirate. He could build an enormous pirate fleet in the period, which made his army stronger over legitimate sovereigns, governments and private military in the time. Only a handful of pirates were able to achieve this feat. In addition it was possible to stop pirates and still live a comfortable lifestyle while gaining the riches.

Peter Easton's fame as a pirate did not an image of a savage beast determined to cause havoc on the sea, but rather an extremely competent officer in the navy proficient in leadership, trade and manners. The man was often praised as a superb navigator, brave, bold and clever who was able to make the most of the ships and crews which he was a part of. His skills allowed him to build a formidable group of people around him which allowed him achieve ever-expanding objectives while remaining in contact to the English crown, who has made many attempts to forgive him and detach his potentially deadly influence off the water.

The first few days of Peter Easton, who would become one of the most effective pirates of the time However, they are not well-known. His family was that had a record of protecting his country's English crown, taking part in the Crusades as well as participating in numerous battles on the sea with his fellow pirates in the Spanish Armada. The first sea-going adventures he was known to have began in 1602 when he was commissioned as an pirate for Elizabeth I of England to protect his English commercial fishing sector in Newfoundland against Spanish invasions. He helped to support English shipping in those days and also hounded Spanish fishermen and traders. Harbour Grace, the

Newfoundland serving as his headquarters operationally, and his flagship was decorated with the Saint George's Cross as a ornament on his ship.

On the 23rd of June, 1604 James I succeeded Elizabeth I changing the course of numerous English privateers their lives. James I quickly filed in for peace in the midst of England as well as Spain. The result was that every pirate was immediately without work which was why they immediately turned to their favorite pastime with a passion: the piracy.

Peter Easton was a pirate who would continue to attack Spanish ships as well as other vessels throughout the Atlantic as if nothing occurred, and immediately transformed him into the pirate. He wasn't satisfied with only the Atlantic coastline close to Canada. He continued to harass Spanish vessels, within the Mediterranean to search for treasure and gold that could be resold in pirate-friendly havens located in the West Indies, with the aid of the wealthy Canadian Killgrew family. In order to increase his fortune and attract more fishers for his pirate crew He began actively attacking English enemies after the size of his fleet increased to an armada comprising ten pirate vessels.

Easton was believed to have been a popular pirate. He sacked over thirty ships in a single piracy operation, stealing a an impressive amount of loot as well as a number of valuable hostages. One of them had even been assigned the task of getting Easton and his crew an official pardon from England. At the time Harbour Grace was granted an official pardon Easton was already relocating to the Barbary Coast and was still fighting the Spanish. At that time the pirate "crew" had expanded into the size of a army of 1500 people. Easton was able to execute even more daring strategies due to this army and also a massive assault against the Spanish tray fleet at waters of the Azores. It is difficult to remember the exact details of the war, but we know that Easton abruptly arrived at the coast of Tunisia afterward and brought with him immense fortune and four enormous Spanish galleons.

Peter Easton was known as one of the most dangerous and most skilled corsairs that engaged in battle against Spain throughout the period that he was involved. Peter Easton amassed an largest fortunes in the history of piracy within just a couple of years. His sea exploits were unrivaled and never was hampered or losing battles against numerous fleets that were sent to pursue his smugglers. The English pardon ultimately struck Easton while he was anchoring within Villefranche, Savoy, which at the time was regarded as a port and was a safe haven for pirates following several prosperous years of sailing. Easton decided to take the pardon. It was accepted by the Earl of Savoy and was keen to profit from the wealthy Easton and immediately purchased a house, earned the title "Marquis of Savoy," and was even able to find an unmarried wife. The Easton remained in Savoy and served as the duke of Savoy until 1620. Then, history disappeared from his life, as per the documents that survived. There is no way to know the manner in which Peter Easton spent the rest of his time or the date or when he died.

Pirate captains often employed tactics of theatrical intimidation throughout the Golden Age of Piracy to create chaos and panic. The most successful methods of this type was flying the pirate flag when the ship approached shore, which allowed the defense personnel time to comprehend the seriousness of their dilemma completely. Captain Peter Easton popularized an unmodified version of the pirate flag, an unmodified black flag prior to the time that "Jolly Roger" flags became widespread and started to contain a variety of dangerous ornaments such as skulls, weapons and bones.

Chapter 6: What exactly is the definition of a pirate?

In reality, a pirate is someone who employs the force of robbery to take over vessels at sea. As you may or might not know it is true that they are criminals but throughout time there have been instances where the law was not enforced and the activities of pirates were openly endorsed by Queens, Kings as well as politicians, as long as it served their purposes.

This book is exploring the pirates who occupied the Caribbean between the years 1600 and 1750. At the time, life was extremely difficult for everyone and youngsters as young as five years old worked for all day long for no gain, and their lifespan was just 40 years. Many people enlisted in navy service as volunteers in order to escape the harsh life they had lived, but frequently they were beaten by an "press-gang" and virtually imprisoned aboard a vessel. Press-gangs would typically employ clubs to knock out men and then carry them to the vessel.

Press-gang members at work forcibly bringing men onto on a vessel.

Pirates.

The experience of a cruise ship sailors of all kinds was awful and gruelling, as we'll soon discover. They were paid very little and terrible food. They also suffered from sickness and dangers were always there. It's no surprise that many of them became frustrated and decided that they would be better off working on their own.

The majority of pirates began their careers as sailors. So they experienced living at sea, as well as working in the sea. A lot of them were veterans of war, and were accustomed to combat. They also desired to live a more comfortable life, and also had greater wealth.

This is the way Hollywood portrays pirates. They weren't always this neat!

In their pirate roles, they frequently took collective decisions regarding managing the ship and also decided between themselves on what ships they would attack. The proceeds were also distributed to ensure they were happier than normal sailors. Their position situated close to islands of the Caribbean was that they were able to enjoy better meals.

Buccaneers

When reading about pirates there is a chance that you will be introduced to the word "Buccaneer". Buccaneers are French sailors who had leapt off a on a ship, and then decided to stay on the shores of the Caribbean or in some island. With a solid understanding of the ocean and sailing the sea, some became pirates. They came up with a method to attract ships. This earned them the name.

The term "buccaneer" comes from an older French word, Boucanier. It describes the process of grilling meat in a flaming burning. They were extremely skilled at hunting wild boar as well as goats and cattle employing long knives that could eliminate the beasts. They made a wood-fired barbecue that prepared the animal's meat. Ships passing by would be able to observe the smoke, or even smell the cooked meat and make a move to get closer hoping to purchase some. If they could get near enough, the pirates would take over the vessel and seize the vessel and the precious goods.

Privateers

A few ships received an official letter of authorization from the country's authorities, which was referred to as the "Marque of letters", that allowed them to take on and destroy vessels of an other country, in particular when the nations were in conflict. On board, the sailors weren't paid any salary and could only keep around 50% of the profits. The major difference between pirates and privateers was the fact that the privateers had protection at ports which were in the hands of their own country, whereas pirates were only considered criminals and could have been hanged had they been found guilty.

"What was the Pirates code?"

In the Navy the rules and regulations were strictly enforced in order to ensure order. Instructions were given from governments, to Admirals, then Captains, and on to the youngest sailor. Pirates had their own rules, and generally, they chose to become pirates. Therefore, each ship was given its own code of conduct. The Captains were usually the ones in control. They were referred to as Articles they were their form as a set of guidelines that pirates had to sign prior to being allowed to join the vessel. These included things such as the way in which decisions were made, how punishment was handed to those who violated the rules; there was no fight among them; making sure the weapons they used were in order and the percentage of any profits they could collect. In some ways, it could be more democratic than what was happening that was enforced on Navy vessels.

Life at Sea

Consider a mixture of a market for fish, an agricultural yard, stinky socks and toilets all in one. It was quite disgusting. There was not much drinking water, so the washing process other than seawater could have been considered an extravagant luxury. The majority of the pirates would've were filthy and dirty.

The boat itself was built from timber. The spaces between planks were "caulked," which means that they were filled with hemp fibres as well as Tar. Even though this did the job fairly well however, there was always a little liquid leaking in which ended up at the lower part of the vessel within the bilges. Without a place to go, it sat and became quite smelly. Therefore, the farther down it went down, the stronger of the stagnant water in the bilge it was possible to smell.

To have fresh, wholesome meats to eat the ships often kept alive animals aboard that resulted in significant amount of manure. this is where the smell of a farmyard originates. Additionally, there was no bathroom in the ship, so if one required to use the bathroom, you needed be seated on a platform hanging over the side of the vessel and let it all fall to the ocean. Also, consider the factor that the Caribbean is a hot region which would add to the horrible smell.

Drinks and food

A few of the most poetic tales of life in the pirate world showcase lavish dinners and a bounty of food and drinks. However, in reality, sailors had to eat the ration of "hard-tack," as well as dried meat. It was impossible to make fresh bread aboard a ship, therefore the crew was given "hard-tack," which were crackers that were dry and comprised of flour, water occasionally fat.

Chapter 7: Did you even know?

There are many stories of sailors who slap their tacks against the table to get rid of the worms. These are the tiny insects who had been buried in the biscuit as it was being kept.

The availability of meat was also limited in availability, so they often needed to use dried pieces of meat that resembled leather take in. In the case of pirates in the Caribbean while they were at sea on any of the islands, they most likely got some food fresh from the sea. Drinking water was an additional issue. Every sailor had around one litre of water every day, which is quite a bit given the humid climate, putting in a lot of effort and sweating heavily. They were also permitted to consume the rum. Rum is often blended with water to make tasting of the water better. Also, it was beneficial in a different manner, as the alcohol contained in Rum killed some of the bacteria within the drinking water.

Hardship

Being on a ships was not easy for various reasons. Storms that were tropical turbulent seas, rough waves and leaking timbers made sure that the ship was wet for the majority times. The simple act of sleeping was difficult. Pirate ships were active and fighting machines. That meant any space was stuffed with ammunition for guns and other stores. This left nothing for extravagant bed sheets! If you're lucky, you may find a spot over the top of an older sails, where you can sleep.

The canon of a ship had to be in use in all instances.

In the 1600s, the navy began introducing hammocks on the ships. Some pirates might have set up an equivalent system on board too. Most hammocks hang on the ceiling of the gun deck so that the sailors could be ready for any situation that came up.

Hot, sweltering moist conditions create the ideal conditions for undesirable guests, such as fleas. They can thrive and reproduce inside any tiny crack, or inside the fibres of canvas as well, and it was hard to find any ship on the water that was uninfested. Fleas can also be adept at jumping over long distances. It was highly likely that everybody who was aboard could be infected.

Rats also were a major issue, and not just could they survive in cramped and filthy areas of the vessel, but they also ate lots of the foods consumed by the crew. This caused contamination of the food.

"Why wear an eye patch?"

Splinters of flying during battle as well as other accidents caused eyes to become vulnerable to infection. Particularly with the number of insects, food waste and the phlegm that sat onboard. Eye patches are a simple method to remove dirt from their eyes. Hence, they were commonly put on by pirates.

Eye patches are often used to shield eyes from injuries.

Disease and health

Drinking and eating in poor conditions food and drink, rat and flea infestations, as well as a lack of sanitation resulted in infection and poisoning from food were quite common along with sea-sickness. in the absence of modern treatments, these can be fatal. In the event of a battle with other vessels, there was the extra dangers associated with any maritime combat. Being shot. Affected by flying wood splinters or being injured by the hand-to-hand combat which would take place. If you happened to suffer a serious injury the odds were very low for a doctor who was a certified expert at the scene, which means the chances of surviving were very slim.

A classic picture of a pirate including an eye-patch and peg leg

"Did pirates really have peg legs?"

Battles in the sea were brutal and there were a lot of injuries So pirates frequently did suffer limb loss. Amputations were not uncommon as well as the fact that there was no anaesthetic, so the patients would be wide awake during surgery. A lot of people would have died from an infection that developed after surgery. In the event that the pirate recovered it was straightforward for the carpenter of the ship to build a 'peg leg made of wood and then pad the entire thing with soft fabric. Though it's not the most attractive thing but it could have allowed the crew to move around while still completing some tasks while onboard.

Why the Caribbean?

The clear blue sky, the clear waters and a warm climate weren't the only reasons pirates adored the Caribbean.

What was it that made the Caribbean which made it an ideal place for pirates to thrive? Pirates weren't simply there to enjoy a wonderful destination to enjoy a holiday but there were other factors, which were linked to greed, history, and the possibility of a better life.

History

Shortly after Columbus was able to discover the 'New World', the huge possibilities that this discovery could provide meant that European nations that had strong maritime tradition fought each other to conquer different parts of the globe.

Spain, France, England and Holland All were involved in the same race. 1509 was the year that Spain discovered what is today commonly referred to as Panama which is located in west of the Caribbean. In a mere 12 years, their explorations led to the discovery of gold and silver.

Today, in what is now known as Mexico Aztecs were created the most gorgeous jewelry made of silver and gold as well as jewellery.

The Spanish Conquistadors, who were the troops who participated in these missions saw it as an opportunity to profit to acquire as much this as possible. The result was the Spanish full-time invasion of the Aztec land, and acquiring the valuable metals.

The most devastating side effect of this was the fact that invading Europeans introduced ailments that were never experienced by locals prior to. With no natural immunity, huge populations of people died. The survivors had a slim chance of surviving the heavily armoured Spanish soldiers.

Along with traveling North to Mexico There were also those who travelled to the south, which is now Columbia, Venezuela and Peru. While traveling further to the south, they encountered an Inca civilisation. Like the Aztecs from Mexico The Incas created beautiful jewelry as well as other items made from local silver and gold and suffered the exact similar death. They died from illnesses they'd never encountered before. Then, the Spanish were able to take over the entire area and were able to help them to get their hands on the precious metals, such as gold and silver jewelry.

In the same way that Portuguese explorationists had encroached on Brazil while French and English explorations had expanded to North America and Canada, it is clear that Spaniards discovered the richest areas.

The Spanish Main

The importance of the Caribbean increased, Spanish interest and influence within the region grew. The ships that came regularly into the Caribbean from Spain carrying supplies as well as luxury items to colonies across the region after they had disposed of their goods, they were able to fill up with gems, silver, gold and spices, tobacco as well as chocolate, to make the return journey back to Spain.

The expansion of vast areas of the coast of the Caribbean eventually became known by the name of Spanish Main. When the Conquistadors began to move to the interior, they took over a vast part of the area that is now today is USA, Mexico, Central America, Columbia, Venezuela and Peru was brought into Spanish administration.

This map from the past illustrates how the Spanish Main and the main ports that are located around the Caribbean

Greed

The entire continent of Europe there was a time where the wealthy were incredibly rich, with a large share part of their land and vast estates and even houses. But the vast majority of the population was severely poor and just barely enough to support them and their families. Therefore, it's not a big surprise to find an abundance of discontent.

The sailors working for so long on merchant vessels, under difficult circumstances, with no pay could be rewarded with the richest and powerful traders becoming wealthy with their expenses. It's easy to imagine why they may be attracted to take a leap of faith and be pirates and possibly earning plenty of money them.

In the opposite end of the spectrum, there were King, Queens as well as Governments and Merchants all vying for their part of the profits from the colonies. In the end, greed was effecting everybody in some way or other.

England has fought and defeated in the Spanish Armada in 1588, but it was nearly bankruptcy. It was thought that Spain helped itself get every bit of silver and gold of and around the New World was both annoying and embarrassing. England was openly supportive of any move towards the Spanish treasure vessels by allowing privateers to take on the ships. The proceeds from these assaults could be retained by the crew members, while the remaining portion was remitted to the Government

Opportunity

The climate and the geography have a significant role to play in the story. As ships leave Spain for westward travel through the Atlantic they travel toward the south-west so that they can catch the trade winds. This brought them toward South America . After entering the Caribbean it is common for the wind to tend to shift counter-clockwise.

After they loaded the vessels for their return journey the ships would depart towards the North of the Caribbean The ships would later pick up Westerly wind that would bring the ships on their way back Europe.

The initial Spanish ports were built on islands. Later, expanding their reach there were several important Spanish colonies were built within the Caribbean There were Havana as well as Santiago de Cuba on the island of Cuba; Cartegena in what is today Columbia; Maracaibo in northern Venezuela as well as Panama City located in Panama.

Privateers, pirates and buccaneers thus had numerous chances to loot the vessels. Once they reached the Caribbean they were loaded with goods of high-value coming from Europe and would easily be sold to Europeans living in colonies. Additionally, they had an excellent worth. Of even more value was the goods they carried that returned. At the point they had filled up with gold, the like, silver, gems as well as sugar, tobacco and many other commodities, they became extremely attractive potential targets.

Chapter 8: The Golden Age

While pirates have operated across history, the period between 1660 and 1726 has been called the "Golden Age' of piracy within the Caribbean.

It was a time of slavery for more than 100 years. In the beginning, Spanish Conquistadors compelled native people to work for them. Later, they began bringing slaves into from Africa. A lot of them worked on the sugar plantations. However, many were sent for work in the silver and gold mines.

The result was increasing the quantity of silver and gold made, as well as more valuable freights headed back to Europe.

Spanish galleons are often well-armed to safeguard their precious cargo.

The time was when Spain was trading with Manila to the west. Ships traveled across the ocean from Acapulco in Mexico up to the Philippines through to the Pacific Ocean, and again the trade winds as well as westerly winds from the Pacific Ocean were used by sailors. Silver was a valuable commodity in China therefore during this voyage out, the ships carried silver. The valuable spices were re-introduced from the east, towards Acapulco then transported via land to be loaded on vessels returning to Spain

In the second quarter of the 17th century Europe was almost in continuous state of war every country working to conquer their neighbors. In the Caribbean it resulted in ships from different nations would often be fighting one in a war of aggression, which resulted in pirates, buccaneers, as well as privateers were always busy.

Safe Havens for Pirates

Certain islands were in Spanish control. A lot of them also included forts, strong defences and therefore pirates could stay far away. All over throughout the Caribbean there were tiny ports, islands and inlets that pirates could use to repair their boats as well as replenish supplies of food and get fresh water. Additionally, there were ports which were safe zones for privateers, pirates and buccaneers. They were controlled by English, French or Dutch colonists. None of them preferred the Spanish. A lot of the refuges were strategically located in the Caribbean. This allowed pirates to strike vessels coming from Europe and the ones returning filled with precious cargoes.

Hispaniola, Tortuga and Haiti

Hispaniola was the name attributed to the entire island which currently is known as"the Dominican Republic at the Eastern part in the East, and Haiti at the Western end. Tortuga is an island of a small size situated off the northern coast of Haiti. It was initially inhabited by the English and then by the Spanish followed by the English then in 1642, it was occupied by French pirates. It was a haven for pirates, especially those who were known as"the "Brethren of the Coast". They were composed made up of French as well as English pirates that often were in a band. The number of pirates they had increased many pirates also relocated to Haiti and began to build new ports for pirates at Port de Paix, and Port au Prince.

Jamaica.

Jamaica is perhaps most well-known due to the pirate's base in Port Royal, which is near modern-day Kingston. It was initially occupied by the Spanish however, in 1655 it was acquired by the English who used it into a base for English as well as Dutch privateers. Governors of the time, at that time, welcomed buccaneers from Tortuga to make use of Port Royal as their base which is why many of the "Brethren of the Coast" were relocated to Jamaica. The most well-known pirates who used Port Royal as their base was Captain Henry Morgan.

The Island of Jamaica. Port Royal is the pirate's base. Port Royal is on the southern coast.

The Bahamas

To the north, there was further to the north, were Bahamas The port of Nassau situated on New Providence Island New Providence was another safe refuge. The port was better positioned to strike ships as they made returning to Europe. There were many well-known pirates that used

Nassau as their base such as "Blackbeard", "Calico Jack Rackham" and Anne Bonney

Truth, Myth and Legend

There are numerous tales about pirates that are many of which are true, while others are fictional. From the time of Robert Louis Stevenson's novel "Treasure Island" we have been aware of pirates. Recent years have seen the fascination with the Hollywood film adaptations of "Pirates of the Caribbean" is causing the growth of curiosity. Let's try to understand all of the stories about pirates.

Walking the Plank

"Did they really get people to walk the plank?"

It's probably just fiction. What is the reason pirates would spend the effort of putting a plank in its proper position? All they had to do was to just throw someone into the ocean.

There were a variety of penalties that pirates used like slaps with the dreadful whip called"Cat-O'nine tails, "Cat-O'nine tails", and "marooning" which is when the individual was thrown in a tiny island, usually the sand bank with just a single bottle of water, and a firearm. The result was really an execution.

The walk of the plank has probably never was a reality.

Earrings

The use of earring was also used by pirates and there are two plausible theories. The first is that, if an sailor was to slip into a pond and drown, the person who found his remains could sell the earring to be able to pay for an appropriate funeral.

Another explanation is been based on it being the case that there exist points of acupuncture on the earlobe which can improve the eyesight. Since pirate vessels were typically not equipped with lights during nighttime and improved sight would be a plus. There is a good chance that the ships that traded in the region of China, Japan, and the Philippines crews might be aware of this tradition with Asian sailors.

Treasure to be found in the treasure chest

Pirates are often the ones who steal precious metals, jewels and gold But what happened to it?

"Where is all the buried treasure?"

There are not many stories of pirates actually digging up their riches. A majority of the loot could likely have come made up of merchandise instead of actual coins which makes it more likely they would have sold the items when they got to port and spent any cash they earned.

Additionally, they were sailing across the Caribbean And we don't know when they'll come back to the same location, which means most likely, they carried their wealth along.

Naturally, there are periodic reports of treasure located in the Caribbean However, this may be more to do that sink in storms and their cargo being discovered by divers as opposed to having anything to do with pirates who bury their hoards of riches.

Pieces of Eight and Doubloons

The Spanish carried the silver onto ships returning to Spain and produced huge silver coins, with an equivalent value of 8 Reals. These coins were also known by the name of "peso de ocho" which means "piece of eight". Treasure ships that were bound to the home port were often carrying massive amounts of these coins and were frequently mentioned in films and stories about pirates for decades afterward.

Other popular pirate currency included Doubloons The coins were constructed from gold and valued around 4 times the value of an eight-piece piece. Therefore, pirates preferred to find Doubloons in a treasure chest whenever they pounced on a ship.

West-Country Accents

Since the first screen version "Treasure Island", pirates were depicted with an accent from the west. The pirate ship with a crew of nearly 50% the crew as having a connection to Devon However, it wasn't the norm.

Pirates were likely to have been from low-income families and could have dialects that were local to the area however, the majority of them came originally from Scotland, Ireland, and London. The southern coast of England included many major seaports including Plymouth, Southampton, and Portsmouth therefore there are probably numerous sailors from the region.

Famous Pirates of the Caribbean

In the early 17th century, it was reported that there were around 2400 pirates and privateers as well as buccaneers working in the Caribbean. Pirate ships typically required between 60 70 to 70 crew members to run them. This means there were likely to be anywhere from 30 to 100 pirate vessels operating in the region.

Certain Captains were very famous and well-known and we will mention some of them here as well as tell us a little about their life. Five men and two ladies that were famous in the time.

Sir Francis Drake. (Privateer)

Portrait of Sir Francis Drake

Many people have heard about Sir Francis Drake, as he is remembered in the history books as being the person who was playing bowls at Plymouth Hoe when the Spanish Armada was spotted. Also, he is remembered for his journey around the globe.

Though he predates to the "Golden Age" of piracy but his story gives the evidence of how privatization began at the Caribbean.

Born in Devon which is located in England circa 1540 however, he and his family moved to Kent. At the age of a young teen the young man began work in merchant vessels then gradually advancing through in the ranks until he became Captain.

At the age of 25 years old, he was operating his own vessel, the intention of establishing genuine trade with Caribbean. However, his vessel was sunk with Spanish Treasure ships, so the ship became a privateer. He retaliated for his actions through the attack of many Spanish ships and attack their ports. The story also tells of his attack on an armed group called the "Silver Train", which is the title given to the wagons which carried the silver across land from the mines of Peru up to the coast of Panama. It resulted in taking a huge amount of silver. The Spanish earned him the title of "El Draque" which translates into "The Dragon".

In 1577, he began his long journey around the world and in particular to explore the western coasts of South America.. The mission was given to him by job from

Queen Elizabeth 1 who was adamant to turn off from fighting Spanish vessels and port wherever the expedition progressed. Then he returned to England three years later, and a new ship "The Golden Hind", and another ship filled with valuable treasure.

In the following years, England was at the war with Spain Then Sir Francis Drake played an important part in the fight against Spain's Armada. He continued his attacks on Spanish ships but ultimately contracted dysentery while during Panama and died in 1596. The body was dumped on the ocean.

Chapter 9: Sir Henry Morgan. (Privateer)

Portrait by Capt. Henry Morgan.

Henry Morgan was born in 1635 in South Wales. He was only when the age of 20 when Morgan set out for the Caribbean initially as a worker, then progressed to become a sea captain before 1663.

The man was a privateer who was involved in a number of assaults on Spanish controlled ports as well as Islands. The Governor of Jamaica backed him. governor of Jamaica who gave him his "Letter of Marque" One of these was set to take place at Puerto del Principe, a Cuban ports located in Puerto del Principe but the people who lived there were warned and they were freed with all their possessions. Henry Morgan's privateers hadn't earned as much as they had anticipated, so they required a new area to target. In the time of Henry Morgan, one of the most prosperous cities along the coast in

Panama was Porto Bello it was where much of the Spanish treasure was kept before it was shipped back to Europe.

The downside was the presence of three forts that protected the territory. Henry Morgan led a small fleet of 10 ships, comprising about 500 soldiers. The group launched an unexpected attack at the first fort followed by a second fort. While many of his soldiers were killed and wounded, the Spanish soldiers at the fort's third were amazed that they surrendered which left Henry Morgan and his crew with the freedom to retrieve all important items that were kept within the town. At the time of their departure the fort, they had taken approximately 100,000 'pieces' out of 8'.

Captain Morgan had planned to conduct his next attack on Cartagena, the capital city. Cartagena located on the coast of today's Colombia however, while in a tiny island preparing the attack, a few people in the group became drunk and accidentally ignited the powder that was on his flagship ship, which destroyed the vessel and a large portion of his crew. His assault at Cartagena was never executed. When they came close to the city, the stormy weather that they experienced on the journey had forced several of his vessels to abandon. There weren't enough privateers remaining to take on the highly defended Cartagena.

Captain Morgan was a participant in numerous others successful raids. One of them was an attack on Maracaibo (in Venezuela), as well as later Panama City itself. While captain Henry Morgan was in and not in favour with the English government and even detained and taken to England to be tried at the age of 1672. He wasn't executed, and was later released. He was able to do the same thing that many pirates and privateers could not which was to get in a graceful manner. Then he returned to live in Jamaica and became the owner of a sugar mill, and was appointed Governor of Jamaica until the year 1688 when he passed away in the year 53. He was considered to be one of the most ruthless and successful pirates that he encountered in his lifetime.

Bartholomew Roberts-"Black Bart" - (Pirate)

The man was John Roberts in a small town called Little Newcastle in South Wales in 1682. The details are not well-known about his childhood as well as the time the name was changed to Bartholomew. In 1718, he was working as a mate aboard the sloop. After this, he was on a bigger slave ship. While he was aboard the ship of slaves when they were attacked by pirates on the coast to the west of Africa.

The slave ship had an opportunity to join pirates. Bartholomew Roberts did so.

The captain of the pirate vessel was also an Welshman who was able to discover that Bartholomew was an excellent navigator. Then, shortly afterward incident, the crew of the pirate ship was themselves attacked, and killed by the Captain. Bartholomew Roberts was elected Captain of the pirate ship and their first trip took them to Brazil. In the waters off Brazil the group encountered 42 Portuguese merchant vessels that were waiting to be escorted by armed ships towards Portugal. Captain Roberts took one of the vessels, and frightened the captain into telling him which of the 42 ships held the largest amount of valuable treasure. The treasure ship was taken and ran off with 40,000 gold dollars.

Bartholomew Roberts was well liked for his role as Captain and was known for his exquisite attire. It is said that he was dressed in red trousers, with an sash tied around his waist and a long jacket. He wore a hat with three corners that hung over his head, and he always carried a pistol. Though we tend to consider pirates Rogues and rogues, Captain Roberts did not drink alcohol or tea, and was never a threat to other ships on Sundays. Also, he was well-known for having ceremonies of worship on the ships he commanded. Maybe this was due to with his background in South Wales.

Even though his tenure in the pirate world was brief, lasting only two years, he managed to build and acquire his own fleet of pirate vessels. In 1721, Captain Roberts decided to return to West Africa. He continued to fight and capture ships near the coast from Africa until 1722, when the naval vessel HMS Swallow attacked his ship. The pirate crew were having a party drinking and in a state of disarray. They were unable to put the fight. At the time of battle, Captain Roberts was killed by a "grape-shot" and killed. His team surrendered they did so after throwing their captain's body on the water. In the short time he was pirate Bartholomew Roberts is known as having attacked more than 250 vessels. In the aftermath of his death and burial, he received the moniker"Black Bart. "Black Bart"

Edward Teach - "Blackbeard" - (Pirate)

"Blackbeard" is probably one of the most popular in the world of Caribbean pirates, but there isn't much information about his childhood. There is a possibility to be that the pirate was born circa 1680, then grew up in the vicinity of Bristol within England. It is likely that he travelled across his home in West Indies and served as privateer in

Jamaica in the period in which England was fighting Spain.

At the time of 1716, he had turned into an pirate, and was relocating in 1716 to New Providence Island in the Bahamas where it was among the safe havens for pirates. At the beginning of his pirate life He made it a rule that he would only take on Spanish ships. However, the crew was not pleased with the fact that he allowed British vessels to carry their cargoes in good condition, and certain members of his crew quit his ship.. In 1716, the pirate attacked a huge French slave ship which was then re-equipped equipped with forty guns. The ship was named "Queen Anne's Revenge"

The man was known as the popular nickname "Blackbeard" due to the characteristic of his massive beard that covered the majority part of his face. It was so long and dense that he tied portions of it in ponytails by using ribbons. Then he had the habit of placing fuses lit into the scabbard during fights. This made it appear as if his head was burning and terrified his clients who thought that it was an animal that was a demon. If that weren't enough, he was enormous, more than six feet tall, and extremely sturdy, and equipped with a variety of weapons, including knives, and pistols.

This character gives an impression of just how frightening Blackbeard could be.

The following year or two years "Blackbeard" gradually increased the quantity of ships that were under his command, and continued to strike and pillage any ships passing by. He sailed in 1718 across the eastern coast of Florida and blocked Charleston's port. Charleston and attacked any vessel which came within. In the course of this blocking, he arrested many prisoners, and threatened to kill those who were not given medicines. The drugs eventually arrived and the prisoners were allowed to leave.

The year 1718 began and at the time it was announced that pirates will be pardoned if they surrendered within September. The same time there was a naval officer named Woodes Rogers was emigrating from England to pursue the goal of taking down any pirates who continued to attack vessels within the Caribbean. In that time "Blackbeard" reduced the size of his crew. He also sought, and eventually received a pardon.

There was no doubt when, shortly thereafter likely due to boredness, he returned to the pirate life. He set up a new base for his boats and crew members in the Ocracoke Inlet, which is located in North Carolina, but his place of residence was discovered by the governor of Virginia and made arrangements for a navy lieutenant known as Robert Maynard to take two armoured sloops in order to take on "Blackbeard" and his pirates. The incident took place in November. The navy vessels were battling Blackbeard simultaneously both of them ended up getting stuck on sandy banks. Blackbeard launched a broadside on the vessel of Lieutenant Maynard which wounded and killed several of his crew.

Blackbeard was on the scene, and the crew and he climbed aboard the ship. However, they were surprised to discover that several navy personnel were secluded beneath the decks. When they finally came out, they were engaged in a brutal combat between hand-to-hand.

In the course of this battle when Blackbeard was slain. According to reports, he was killed several times and been wounded by about 20 swords. There is also a rumor that his head was severed and was hung from the bowsprit on the ship of Lieutenant Maynard. An extremely grisly ending for the pirate captain.

Chapter 10: Jack Rackham "Calico Jack" - (Pirate)

A sculptural representation on one of Pirate "Calico-Jack" Rackham.

Jack Rackham was born on the Island of Cuba in 1682. There isn't much revealed about his life before. He was on the water in 1718 under a pirate named Charles Vane. The ship on which they were was a tiny sloop when they encountered an even larger, and also more heavily armed French Warship. Captain Vane chose to withdraw to avoid the French ship. However, Jack Rackham and most of the crew were determined to take on the vessel. They were accused Charles Vane of cowardice, and tried to remove him from the position of Captain. They offered him along with the other crew members who supported them, a small boat to depart on. In the end, Jack Rackham was chosen as the Captain of the ship. "Calico Jack" began by taking on small vessels around the coast.

The nickname was "Calico Jack" was due to the vividly colored Calico shirts he frequently was seen wearing, and soon was renowned for his extravagant fashion sense. The chance of being caught was extremely close in 1719, when he obtained a small English sailing vessel and was in port to purchase supplies. The large Spanish warship was able to spot the pirates but because of the low water was unable to get to the pirates. The night was a nightmare for the pirates "Calico Jack" and some members of his crew removed their possessions from their ship, and hopped on the English sailing vessel that they taken. At dawn, the Spanish warship sank the pirate vessel, and pirates quickly sailed off on the sloop they had stolen.

The amnesty for pirates was granted, and "Calico Jack" and his crew were given pardons. While in port, Calico Jack met and became in love by Anne Bonny, the wife of a local seaman He along with "Calico Jack" stole a sailing vessel, and together with a brand new crew, they went back to pirates. Anne was able to meet a woman named Mary Read who was an skilled swordsman. The woman frightened everyone by dressing as a male, however ultimately, they both were welcomed into the group. While sailing in 1720, Jamaica his vessel and crew were taken by pirate hunters. They were all drinking and did not want to fight and were detained and taken to Jamaica in the hope of being examined and sentenced to execution. "Calico Jack" was hanged in Port Royal on the 18th November. The body of the pirate was placed inside a gibbet that was located in a tiny islet close to the port's entrance in order to serve as an example for others pirates.

Anne Bonny - (Female pirate)

Anne Bonny was born in Kinsale, County Cork, Ireland in 1702. The girl was famous for her the red hair of her mother and an ebullient temper. Her family moved to the Carolinas in the Carolinas, where her father was a millionaire by owning an estate.

A seaman named James Bonny married Anne in an effort to purchase the plantation. He did not succeed, so he sent Anne away to the Bahamas instead. There Anne met and became infatuated with "Calico Jack" Rackham. They fled to sea and lived their lives as pirates. Anne was as ferocious as her fellow pirates She was extremely proficient using cutlasses and pistols. After their vessel was taken Anne was pregnant even though she'd been sentenced to die but she was never seen again. There is a possibility that her rich father gave officials a break who then returned her to Charleston. In Charleston, she got married again and remained married for many years, until she died in the age of 80.

Mary Read - (Female pirate)

This colored engraving depicts the women pirates Anne Bonny and Mary Read.

Mary Read was born in London at the end of the seventeenth century. Her mother wore her in male clothes. The habit of dressing in masculine clothes lasted after she reached a certain age, and she eventually got a job at sea on a ship. As she got older and joined Army and served in the area that is now Belgium. She was a master of the sword. At this point she also met her love her, and then married an Dutch soldier. The couple lived in Holland however, the death of her husband led her to flee for the Caribbean. They continued to wear male clothes, as well as time she was privateer. In 1720, she joined Calico Jack Rackham and Anne Bonny as pirates. Though she was female, she enjoyed the reputation of a warrior and was able to fight like any of the males. After their ship was taken captive, she and Anne Bonny claimed they were expecting, and they were given a pause in execution. It's believed that in the prison, she was struck with fever and then died in 1721.

Chapter 11: The True Origins of Piracy

If you are told stories of pirates and piracy, one of the most likely first image you imagine would be Pirates of the Caribbean. If you are a fan of books rather than films, then you may consider Robert Louis Stevenson's acclaimed novel Treasure Island. No matter if you imagine the Captain Jack Sparrow or Long John Silver The most important thing to remember is that you're looking at pirates from the 17th century. It was a period that is often described as the golden era of piratery. In this period, there were many of the most famous pirates whose actions were the subject of legend however the reality to the truth is they were far removed from the early pirates. The historical records include a myriad of tales about pirates operating in the seas of high-speed from to the period in the time of Ancient Greeks and Romans. One story includes Julius Caesar himself being kidnapped by pirates who demanded ransom. The incident occurred a complete 1600 years prior to when people like Captain Kidd, Blackbeard and Calico Jack even existed!

The idea that pirates are around for a long time may seem odd at first, it is due to our perception of what a pirate is. A lot of people see pirates as a group of adventurers who earn a living by pillaging large merchant vessels. After they've accumulated their money, they set off to the shore, and revel in every pleasure they can get from gold. It's true up to a certain extent, however generally, it is just a figment of imagination. What is the truth in this is that pirates nothing more than pirates who are outlaws in the sea. Pirates' ships are not different from a group of thieves who rob pedestrians. So, as theft is a crime that is as old as records from the past, it shouldn't come as a surprise that pirates have such a long history of origins too. When mankind began to venture to sea the pirates came into the story.

As with any other group of time, pirates made their mark at different time periods and different ways. The Venetians faced their own pirate threat during their time in the Adriatic Sea several hundred years before the golden age pirates. Settlements of pirates in the Dalmatian coastline almost affected the Venetian commerce through maritime, which meant that the survival of Venice was dependent on elimination of Dalmatian criminals. This was just another episode in the history of pirates, however each civilization that depended on trade through the sea must confront the menace of criminal opportunists, who considered merchant vessels that were not guarded as an opportunity to make money fast. In the past, Greece as well as her island civilization, was yet another wealthy civilization that was required to deal with the problem of theft from maritime vessels to preserve their status as a world-class superpower. It is true that any culture or nation with a fleet of merchant vessels also faced the problem of pirates.

The fact that pirates are tracked back to the very beginnings of humanity can make it much easier to think there is a possibility that Knights Templar could be connected to the piracy. A second important aspect to take into consideration to consider is the attitude of pirates. The majority of pirate teams were composed of skilled sailors and fighters that had fallen from favor or just wanted to live an easier living. A life aboard a ship for trade wasn't a pleasant one. Indeed, people who worked on merchant ships typically received no more than slave pay. If you think about the hardships they were subjected to and the wealth that their patrons were earning the world, it's not surprising that tensions were as widespread and as widespread. It's also the case for sailors, who frequently were forced to live in such extreme circumstances that they were thought to be less cared for than prisoners. These miserable working conditions were most often the primary reason an experienced sailor might choose to pursue the path of pirates and piracy, despite the fact that the sentence for pirates captured was the death sentence.

Political instability was also the reason for the large amount of pirates' crews. If kings or nations couldn't afford to maintain large navy fleets and they were forced to remove numerous vessels from the service of their vessels, which left their crews unemployed. Instead of going back to their home, with their expertise unusable, they would seek alternatives at sea. A lot of them would work as mercenaries in different kingdoms which might not have an adequate navy, while some took up a path to the life of pirates. The period of the golden age of pirates, there was a difference between pirates and paid naval merchants. The ships who received an order from a foreign government to attack a specific country's vessels were referred to as privateers. If they stayed true to the specifics of their agreement, they could be considered legal. The concept of mercenary vessels is crucial in establishing the connection between Templar Knights with piracy. After the Templars ended their existence, they needed use their expertise into action in any way they could. As many new orders were formed, of knights and mercenaries, some changed into pirates or mercenaries in keeping with an old-fashioned tradition for fighters and sailors who were suddenly out of a job that paid.

Chapter 12: The Legend of the Templar Pirate Fleet

It is possible that what's difficult to understand about the link between pirates and Knights Templar could be the maritime part of the idea. In the end it is true that there was a sea. Knights Templar was a renowned group of Crusader Knights that had been trained and armed for battle in the land. It is believed that they disappeared from the scene but then reappeared as the infamous pirates in the Caribbean is quite different from what one would think. There were other military units that had disintegrated at times, usually to be mercenary forces or similar. Greek generals were often generals of mercenary forces after the conflicts were finished, which demanded the aid of very well-armed and well-trained forces. What justification would the Knights Templar need to be an ocean-based power, where their fighting skills will be useless? This is the answer in a variety of intriguing facts regarding the Templar breakup.

The primary fact that lends an explanation for that of the Knights Templar becoming pirates is that the Templars owned a fleet 18 vessels in south France during the time of their demise in the middle of 14th century. Although 18 ships might not appear to be a huge deal in the present, the fact is that the expense of maintaining these vessels was quite a burden during that period. Particularly in light of the fact the fact that they were galleys that were designed for battle. Warships could only be useful in the event of a war that was being waged in the ocean, so what purpose would the fleet serve after the Templar orders were disbanded? As the king of France took over Templar territories, one would imagine that he'd taken over the Templar fleet or even burned it down. There is, however, no evidence of this occasion. Instead it appears that the Templar fleet vanished, as did a lot of those who pledged an allegiance towards the Order.

A different interesting aspect is some of the areas where survivors of Templars discovered new residences. The fact that the Templar order broke up didn't mean that members would have to change into farmers, or another kind of worker that was non-militant. A lot of the remaining Templars were able to find a new home within other groups of that time like those of the Knights Hospitallers. In addition, a number of Templars established new orders which was essentially a continuation of their tradition and the only difference was their name. recognized as. The most fascinating aspect of these new orders is the places that they came from. They were founded by the Order of Christ, for instance, was a brand new organization that was founded in Portugal which was a place that would which was to soon be known for its maritime achievements. Actually, Portuguese sailors were to be praised for their achievements in the coming hundreds of years. Malta was a second location that was that was chosen by the Templars as their future residence. Incredibly, Malta would soon become known for its acts of piracy versus other sovereign countries.

A different aspect that can aid in understanding the link between pirates and Knights Templar is that prior to the Templar dissolution, the Pope had a large say over European trade on land as well as at the sea. Thus, any maritime commerce that wasn't directly under the authority and safeguards of the pope would effectively be referred to as piracy since it could be considered to be illegal. In the end, the main reason the Papacy was responsible for trade in the past was to make sure that the merchants were able to share in the earnings. So, any fleet who did not pay their "tithe" to the church was considered outlaws or, since maritime pirates were known as pirates.

It is believed that Templars could be involved in trade maritime might seem strange at first glance, but reality is that Templars actually established one of the very first bank methods that have been recorded in the history of mankind. Actually, whenever they weren't busy, the Templar Order wasn't busy trying to take back their Holy Land from the Muslim countries, it was busy enriching its own members through banking, trade as well as land acquisition. The Templar Order did not just pose an imminent threat to the military of any nation that was sovereign, but it was also a financial risk, since it was as robust in terms of finances as it was. So after the Order disbanded, not only did huge numbers of military personnel have to locate new places in which they could practice their trades as well as the entire system of banking, filled with huge amounts of treasures, gold and other assets of great value. The Papacy was requesting that these documents and assets be transferred to other Orders that were dependent on the Pope but it was never done. Instead, the assets from the Knights Templar simply disappeared, as did a huge fleet of vessels that could transfer such wealth securely and quickly. The fact that these vessels would remain in commercial capacity, or perhaps harassing ships in the supervision of the Papacy in and of itself, doesn't take much of imagination to consider.

Chapter 13: Legends of the Templar Knights in the Americas

Columbus Day is a holiday commemorating the achievements of Christopher Columbus that is still being celebrated across the United States today. One of the reasons it is being celebrated is the fact that it's become a custom to observe it. Modern studies have revealed the fact that Christopher Columbus had nothing at anything to do with the "discovery" of the New World. It is true that Columbus have the actual experience of discovering his way to the North American continent in his time, but the overwhelming evidence indicates that it existed long before the famed 1492 journey. Although archeological evidence and other historical proof suggests that Vikings actually landed at Newfoundland, Canada, there is evidence to suggest trips into America by the Chinese, Americas from the Chinese or even the Egyptians.

There is however, historical and archaeological evidence suggests the possibility that another people group arrived in the American shores before Columbus, namely the Knights Templar.

Many stone carvings have been found across North America which are eerily identical to the symbols that were used by the Templar Order until its end. The most notable was that of the Templar Cross, a symbol exclusive for the Templar Order that can't be misinterpreted once you understand the shape. Although some might suggest it is an actual cross, the reality is that the symbols were extremely important during the times during the time of Templars. Every knight's order would be able to identify its own symbol typically a variant of the Cross to represent the group's Christian religion, which differed in its design. This was important because the symbol was often the most important way knights in the field were able to distinguish between different groups. Thus, every symbol should look distinctive and distinct the same way that modern flags vary from the other. Thus, any symbol that includes a cross at all like the one utilized for the Knights Templar must be carved by an Templar Knight, or anyone who paid tribute to the Knights Templar.

Another convincing piece of evidence supporting the Templar presence within the Americas before Christopher Columbus can be found in Scotland. Within the city of Roslin there's a chapel, Rosslyn Chapel, which is well-known due its connection to it being the site of Da Vinci Code. It was built in the 15th century. this church was already utilized long before Columbus ever thought of traveling to the Americas. However, inscribed on the limestone ceiling of the chapel are pictures of maize, which is a plant that is only found only in the Americas. It is a matter that has been a source of concern for the historians. For instance, how could the architects have been aware of an existing construction site while the New World was yet to be explored? Many theories were offered to discredit the findings However, what makes the discovery even more convincing is that the man who was responsible for directing the building of the chapel is William Sinclair, 1st Earl of Caithness. This is significant in the fact that William Sinclair was a Mason as well as a descendant with that same name would go onto become the grand master of Scotland's Freemasons. The connection between Freemasons with the Knights Templar is the subject of numerous books, films and heated discussions. It is interesting that some Templar symbolisms and designs are also found in Rosslyn Chapel only adds to the possibility that Templars may not just have played a role in the building of the chapel, and that they also were in charge of the designs that may have been derived from the knowledge gained by studying the Americas.

The most important question isn't how the Templars had the ability to complete journey towards North America. North American continent, but more about the reason. The Americas in the time that the Templars were comparatively undeveloped compared to European standards. This meant it was not possible to find trading or financial incentives to establish a base of activities on the New World. In reality, the Templars already had a good financial position, these considerations were not important. In reality, it was the Templar Order was in essence an exiled nation as was those of the Israelites of the Old Testament. So one of the primary goals for the Templar Order was to create an entirely new homeland in the promised place' in which they could come back and bring their glory. Thus, the concept that there was a new world could have been of the utmost significance to the now disbanded Order does not come without merit. Furthermore, as that the Templar Order was in possession of an enormous collection of vessels that could travel by sea, Not only did they have motivation to make the voyage, but also the resources to undertake this kind of voyage. In all it was there was a chance that the New World would have been among the earliest possible places where a massive amount of people and their resources could disappear with no trail.

Chapter 14: Roger de Flor

The tale of pirates is not full without an iconic person who embodies the spirit of piracy in itself. In all likelihood, what is the golden era of piracy have been without people like Jack Rackham, William Kidd, Henry Avery, Edward Teach and others? They are the ones who gave the picture of piracy during the 17th and 18th century that we have today. Films like Pirates of the Caribbean would be impossible without the historical exploits of these men. It is fortunate that the story of pirates that tells the story of Knights Templar is not without characters of this kind. Roger de Flor, a Templar Sergeant was an officer in the Templar fleet. He was able to make an impression in the latter half of the 13th and the beginning of the 14th century. His charismatic character caused just many problems within the Templar Order as it did in the world outside.

Roger de Flor was born in 1266. This means that it was at the peak of Templar authority and influence. He was also known as the German title, Rutger von Blume, de Flor never became an authentic knight of the order. Rather, his title was Sergeant, which was a higher professional rank. He was an experienced seaman and eventually became a captain of the formidable and revered Templar fleet. But his darker side began to emerge and caused his time as a member of the Templar Order to come to the end of his career. According to eyewitness accounts at the period, de Flor over charged his passengers on the ship that he commanded during the battle of Acre in 1291. De Flor's efforts to make personal gains from Templar enterprise was against two of the fundamental Templar principles. It was firstly not permitted under his Templar code to have all personal belongings other than the items in you have been given in the Order gave you. In addition in addition, it was prohibited to steal cash from the Order as well as to utilize Templar status to gain personal financial wealth.

Instead of disappearing into the shadows, de Flor borrowed a huge sum of money from an Genoese nobleman Ticino Doria. De Flor used this money to purchase a boat and put it to good use with his newly discovered occupation, piracy. As a lot of nations during that time were engaged at war in one way or another, it was very easy for pirates to earn a living by snatching vessels of any nation. This kind of harassment was commonplace when war was in the air because that was what the main goal of any enemy. In addition, it was impossible for any resources to be dedicated to the pursuit of pirates as every resource needed to be employed for the actual battle. De Flor continued this chapter through many years, before finally deciding to make himself more "legitimate and 'professional' by contracting himself as a mercenary mariner and a skilled tactician.

Roger chose to hire his expertise out to the Holy Roman Emperor Frederick, who was also king of Sicily. It was at this time that the Spanish and French kings were fighting for control of Sicily, each fielding a supremely powerful army and navy. This was largely due to the Papal decrees against the Holy Roman Empire, considering them to be heretics and blasphemers. Rather than bringing his professional forces south, Frederick hired mercenary units to stave off the Papal ordered attacks. He hired de Flor as a vice-admiral, giving him almost absolute authority over the Sicilian fleet. De Flor used his skills to great effect until the war's end in 1302. With no war to justify the mercenary forces he was paying, Frederick disbanded all non professional units, meaning that de Flor was once again a free agent.

Just because one war was over didn't mean that there weren't still many more still to be found. De Flor knew this all too well, so rather than packing up and going home he hired himself out once again, this time to the Byzantine Empire. Roger now had a large following of mercenary sailors and soldiers, also unemployed from the end of the Sicilian fight. Arriving in Constantinople in September of 1302, de Flor met with the Byzantine Emperor, Andronicus II, who immediately hired him and his fleet, known as the Catalan Company, which boasted some 6,500 men at arms. Before long de Flor rose in rank, even marrying the emperor's niece, Maria Asenina. He was granted the title of grand duke and made commander-in-chief of the Byzantine army and navy.

De Flor's successes and power eventually caused the Byzantine emperor to become fearful of him. He accused de Flor of serving his own interests over those of the emperor and sought to have him removed from his position. De Flor, already keen on establishing his own principality in the East, sent some men with his fortunes to Magnesia. Upon their arrival, however, de Flor's men were slaughtered and his treasures confiscated by the local people. He laid siege to the town in the hopes of retrieving his treasures, but he never succeeded. He was assassinated by the emperor's son in 1305, after having settled many of his soldiers in different towns throughout Europe and the Middle East. His men avenged his death, raiding Byzantine towns and villages in what has been called the Catalan Vengeance.

Chapter 15: Possible Templar Origins of the Infamous 'Jolly Roger'

Perhaps no single word, symbol or item embodies the golden age of piracy more than the infamous Jolly Roger. The sight of the white skull and crossbones on a black flag instantly raises images of the famous pirates such as Blackbeard and Jack Rackham on their ships searching for their next victim. While the sight of the Jolly Roger evokes intrigue and fascination today there was a time when the sight of that flag caused panic and fear. After all, it was no coincidence that the pirates used a symbol of death on their flag. Any resistance to the high seas marauders would result in the death of all persons aboard the target ship. However, a new theory has arisen which provides a different explanation for the use of the skull and crossbones on the Jolly Roger. It suggests that the purpose was not so much to strike fear and panic in those who saw it, but instead was to identify the true identity of the pirate crew. This new theory traces the symbol of the skull and crossbones back to the Knights Templar themselves.

One piece of evidence that is used to support the idea that the Jolly Roger is a creation of the Knights Templar is the fact that the Templar Order used the symbol of the skull and crossbones elsewhere in their culture. This symbol can be found on numerous Templar tombstones, both in Europe as well as in the New World. While this imagery may seem very sinister and macabre to us today the truth of the matter is that it held a very significant meaning to the Templars. The skull and crossbones was used to remind the Templar Knights that this physical life was temporary, and that death was the inevitable outcome. Additionally, all physical treasures were destined to fall into decay eventually, just as the body would. Therefore, this symbol served to encourage the Templars to pursue the spiritual treasures that would last for eternity. In short, the skull and crossbones was a reminder of the Order's true value system.

Another possible tie linking the Jolly Roger and the Knights Templar is the Templar Cross. As mentioned earlier, each Christian order of knights had their own variation of the cross as their particular symbol or emblem. This symbol was used to distinguish one knight from another, much the same way as a flag on the sleeve of a soldier does today. Therefore, each cross had to be very distinct, as any similarities between different symbols could lead to mistaken identity and much confusion on the battlefield. Subsequently, the Templar Cross was a very unique design, with arms that began narrow at the center and widening out towards the edges. This symbol was used in orders in Malta and Portugal after the Templar Order was dissolved, and the imagery has lasted to this day in such forms as the Portugal National Football Team badge. While the cross itself may not seem to have anything to do with the Jolly Roger all one has to do is to turn the cross at a 45 degree angle and you are left with a symbol that looks all to reminiscent of the crossed bones on the Jolly Roger!

The decision to use the Jolly Roger to identify members of the Knights Templar may seem strange at first. After all, why not simply use the Templar Cross as their symbol? In order to fully understand why the adoption of a different flag makes sense we need to remember that the Templar Order was outlawed by the Pope himself, meaning that any member was fair game for anyone who wanted to do him harm. Thus, to use the Templar Cross would have invited attacks from any nation who was under the direction of the Roman Catholic Church. And, seeing as such powerhouses as Spain and France were very much Catholic, then the last thing any Templar ship wanted to do was to advertise themselves. Therefore, a new flag was very much needed if the order was to recognize one another without necessarily being recognized by would be enemies.

Another important thing to understand is the evolution of flags over the years. Today we are accustomed to flags that mainly have stripes, stars or a mix of the two. However, in the 12th and 13th centuries flags were very different. Symbols defined people and places rather than generic stripes. Many animal motifs were used in flags as a result of the coats of arms given to that place. Therefore, to see the Jolly Roger in the Middle Ages would not have been as out of place as we might expect. Rather, to see a flag with stripes or stars would have been strange to the people of the time. The skull and bones would have been a fairly safe symbol to use as well since the only other place where the symbol could be found was within tombs and churches belonging to the Order. Therefore, only someone who had been in the Order would have had the chance to see the symbol in use.

Chapter 16: Templar Buried Treasure

The best pirate stories are filled with ships, cutlasses, peg legs, and most important of all, buried treasure. Countless people continue to search for buried pirate treasure to this very day, breaking out their trusty metal detector and their countless sources on why Captain Kidd would have buried his gold at that particular place. One of the biggest problems with the notion of buried pirate treasure is that it really doesn't make any sense. After all, any treasure that a pirate crew won at sea was split immediately amongst the crew, acting as the only form of pay that the crew would receive. To bury the treasure would be like your place of work burying your paycheck. It simply doesn't make any sense. Additionally, the notion of pirates actually finding treasure is another misconception of what life was really like as a pirate. For the most part pirates had to settle for unguarded merchant ships, and these would usually be hauling less valuable cargo. Therefore, the average pirate 'treasure' would consist of cloth, oil, silk, lumber and other items of moderate value that would have to be sold at the next port in order to be turned into spendable cash. The idea of pirates hitting a treasure galleon is nothing short of fantasy.

Therefore, the question remains—where did the idea of buried treasure come from? One answer is literature. Again, much of our modern notion of pirates comes from such classic literary works as Treasure Island. These books often spoke of buried treasure and chests of gold coin. While these images are amazing for the imagination, they hold very little historical value. There is one scenario, however, where buried treasure could be a possibility. This scenario is when a pirate ship would know that they would be unable to escape capture from enemy forces. In this case they may choose to transfer all of their valuable cargo to the nearest shoreline where they could bury it, thus keeping it safe from the hands of the authorities who would otherwise seize it. This plan would be a last ditch effort, however, as there would be a huge risk of not being able to find the treasure again. Any makeshift burying of cargo would not leave much time for map making, so the whole notion of 'x marks the spot' is not likely in this situation.

The only way that the idea of buried treasure and a map marking where the treasure is buried makes sense is if the treasure is something that might not be spendable. If, for example, the treasure was something of religious value, then it could be buried for safekeeping, with a map made to keep track of its location for a time when it would be safer and perhaps more appropriate to recover it again. There is a group that this scenario would make sense with—the Knights Templar. One of the enigmas about the Templar Order is its sudden and meteoric rise to wealth and power. How a group that started as eight knights who were supposed to act as an escort for pilgrims to the Holy Land suddenly became the strongest and wealthiest religious order on Earth is still a matter of heated debate. The most popular explanation is that the Templar Knights discovered something while in Jerusalem, something which could change the very foundation of our understanding of Christianity and even God. It is believed that the Papacy paid off the Templars to keep their information secret. It is also believed that this may have been the reason why the Church turned on the Templars in the end, dissolving the Order and commanding that they turn over all of their assets to the Church.

The fact that the Templar fleet of 18 galleys disappeared, along with the Templar wealth, means that the Roman Catholic Church failed to achieve their true goal of obtaining whatever it was that gave the Templar Order its true source of power and wealth. Stories of the fleet fleeing to Scotland and even the New World are numerous and not without evidence. Therefore, if anyone would have reason to bury a treasure, and to do so for long enough to warrant making a proverbial treasure map, it would be the Templar Knights.

Chapter 17: Boarding Axes

The boarding axe as well as the tomahawk is a weapon that could serve multiple purposes. ideal for tackling enemies as well as for cutting off the bulkheads and doors of wooden ships to create locked quarters, where the guards of the vessel can barricade themselves in an boarding exercise. It was efficient in cutting through grappling lines in battle.

Boarding Axes comprised sharp blades on one end and sharp hammers on the other, and they could be attached to a three or two-foot handle. For a weapon, the boarding axe proved difficult to use even for the toughest of opponents and were more effective for their use as tools than an axe for killing men. The pistol or dagger could have proved better than the boarding axe when within close range. Although during boarding, there could be some instances of exceptions. The axe worked most effective when used to cut ropes from the boarding hooks, cut down riggings and masts, and generally to rip through ships made of wood such as doors, decks the hatches and locks.

The boarding axe was also used for tasks that weren't combat-related, but were crucial. They were employed to cut the hot cannon balls are embedded into the hull of ships when fighting. If they were not checked, they could spark fires in the ship's timbers. The boarding axe's broad ends were also utilized to cut down the rigging, and used as a hook that was used to pull the debris and rigging away.

Tomahawks

Tomahawks were a boarding axe's younger sister. They weren't an all-purpose tool but were instead used exclusively for fighting. They could be useful in combat with hands-to-hand or to throw a hatchet. Although they were not ideal for taking doors, they were more convenient to use in close-quarters fights.

Marlinspike

A work piece for ropes The marlinspike was utilized for knot tying or splicing, as well as sewing. In general, six inches or less up to a foot in length, marlinspikes may be bigger than two feet to work on heavy ropes and heavy cables. Marlinspikes are usually made from metal, and iron or steel was the preferred materials. They could be useful for opening the lids of containers, cutting lines, painting chippers and even as hammers.

Like belaying pins, was only used as a flimsy weapon. In the case of an unexpected assault, the marlinspike made by a person who was aware of exactly what they were doing can cause damage in close range. They can be used to be an unintentional dagger, or the skull cracker hammer.

Buckler

A buckler is a tiny shield, ranging from six inches to over one foot wide. It was held with the palm of one hand, then used combination with a sword. It proved effective at preventing attacks from a sword in an actual duel. Deflecting the strike of an adversary permitted pirates to come closer to the ship during fights.

The buckler can also be employed as an offensive weapon to strike an adversary and the shield's metal material would appear as brass knuckles if put on the opponent's stomach or face. It was also effective to bind an opponent's sword and a pirate could to utilize his own.

The word buckler is one of the words from which some historians believe the term"swashbuckler" comes from. The buckler did not work against arrows, firearms and even guns and could only be used for hand-to-hand combat. The buckler fell out of fashion together with sabers, arrows and other bladed weapons when firearms were more widespread as well as more precise and more efficient.

Cutlass

The cutlass was the primary weapon of pirates. It was a narrow wide sword that had the blade having a slight curve that was sharpened at its cutting edges. It was usually a slashing weapon having a cupped or basket to form a guard for the hilt to guard the user against an attack from a counter. The cutlass was a popular ship weapon during the Golden Age of Piracy. Used to deter boarders, or cutting down defenders, the cutlass did not run out of ammunition.

The reason for the cutlass's popularity is not just due to the fact that it could be useful in a combat, but also because it was strong enough to cut into lines, ropes and sails. A short blade cutlass is useful for close quarter fights in which a long, heavy sword could be ineffective.

There are numerous rumors about pirates developed the cutlass however, there's no concrete proof to support that. The cutlass was most popular with pirates due to the fact that using it did not require any formal education.

Dagger

Dagger Dagger was a tiny multi-purpose knife, which was useful to use for a knife or as a killing weapon. The knife was small enough to hide under clothing, and deadly when within close proximity. Daggers were weighed between one and two pounds, and the blade was that was between six and 18 inches. Daggers had an hilt to prevent the hand of the pirate from sliding towards the blade, and also to deflect the sword's blow during fighting. It was designed to attacks that were puncture and thrust and not for slashing as cutlass or sword. Daggers served as a device for cutting ropes as well as sails, meat and even the time of dinner. Daggers were used by nearly all pirates since they were cheap compared to guns and swords at the period.

Dirk

The term Dirk is an Scottish word meaning an extended dagger. Dirks were typically an axe blade that was cut down and mounted to a hilt of a dagger. The primary use of it was for boarding and was beneficial for the thrust of blows. Dirks may be a double or a single blade.

Scimitar

The first scimitars featured an extremely curving half-circle blade. It was also known as"shamshir" or "shamshir" which meant lions tail. Originating from Persia the type of blade was popular throughout Muslim as well as Indian regions of Europe as well as Asia. Its large-scale design blade led to the weapon being become extremely heavy, resulting in an impressive power to strike. However, it was not easy to manage. Close quarters battle on the deck of a vessel or beneath decks could limit force of the scimitars.

The only thing that can be achieved is making the scimitar less powerful, taking away its power to strike. In consequence of this, it was never a main weapon in sea warfare.

Boarding Pikes

Pikes were spears that had a long length that had a handle made of wood as well as a tip made of metal. Naval pikes were shorter variants of pikes referred to as boarders pikes that ranged from four to six feet long. They were employed to deter groups of boarding, but they could also serve for offensive purposes. Pikes for storage included racks on masts of ships.

The pike could be used in a range or melee weapon. Pikes' accuracy is a matter of debate, and it could be useful when accompanied by pirates in battle. The pikes were used for warships, usually in order to deter groups of boarding party members--as late as third quarter of 19th century.

Firearms

Chapter 18: Flintlock Weapons

The flintlock was an flint piece that was stowed between jaws that were attached to the hammer's short length. The hammer was then pulled back to the "cocked" position. Once the trigger was released, the hammer slid out, the hammer that was loaded with springs advances, causing the flint strike an iron piece. The steel piece was known as frizzen. The movement of the flint and the hammer pulled the frizzen away, revealing the covers to let in the food and the gunpowder contained within. The flint was struck by the steel, sparks were produced that slid into the pan, and ignited the powder. The flaming powder will be able to burn through a tiny hole through the barrel of the gun, and spark the primary charge of powder. The explosion will cause the gun to shoot, blasting the ball from the barrel.

Matchlock Weapons

A matchlock gun held an unburning slow-burning match within an end-capsule of a serpentine that was a lever that curved. The lever, or trigger in the later versions was pulled the serpentine moved ahead. After that, the clamp slid down and the mechanism brought the match lower into the flash pan and ignited the primer. The primer's fire traveled through the torch hole sparking the main charge. The match that was burning would need be taken out prior to loading the weapon. The match must be placed back into the clamp. A new one has to be put in and ignited for the purpose of firing the gun once more.

Snaphance Weapons

Snaphance Snaphance is the latest technological advancement of the wheel lock firing mechanism, as well as the precursor of the firing mechanism for flintlocks. The term "snaphance," can be traced back to Dutch and is of Dutch origin. However, it is not possible to say without certainty that the gun was invented in the Netherlands. The mechanism is operated by an flint smashed against a striker's surface in front of a steel pan, that ignites the primer powder that ignites the gun.

The flint can be held by one of the clamps at the top of the cock. As the trigger is pulled, the cock is moved forward by the tension of the spring. The cock then hits the steel plate or frizzen. The impact would cause sparks as the steel heats up and release shavings. They would then fall into the pan, and then spark the primer. The flash of light travels through a gap in the core charge of powder, which causes it to ignite. It discharges and a shot goes down the barrel before exiting the muzzle.

Pistols

Following their swords that were a popular weapon of pirates, and also the ones for which they're most famous for. The pistols of the time usually fired just one shot before having to be loaded again, however there were variations (see Multi barreled guns) however, they were extremely light in weight. Since reloading during the heat of a boarder's action is not a viable option, pirates had to take several pistols in battle. Blackbeard as well as Black Bart were renowned for their belts full of guns.

They were not effective beyond a close range, and the smaller the gun, the less precise they proved to be. There was the option of having a few pistols of varying sizes or just a handful of larger pistols. However, smart pirates will have a sword or knife to use when their guns ran out.

Musket

The musket was a predecessor of the rifle, and was is a weapon more often used in pirate vessels as opposed to cannons. Cannons, when shot with precision, can destroy a pirate vessel, but a single shot may cause it to sink. In the case of pirates who pursued a fleeing ship, their goal was not the vessel itself. The focus was on the crew. Pirates are often viewed for their crack-pot abilities. They could reduce the amount of opposition they encountered from a vessel carrying merchants even before they started to embark by removing the crew. A musket would be perfect for this job.

The first time firearms were used they were put to use at points blank range or even in the form of a firing volley. They weren't the most precise. The musket was the very first attempt to make a firearm that had precision. Muskets with a matchlock were used as well as later

Flintlock ones were also available. They measured four feet or larger in length, and they weigh close to twenty pounds, so they were difficult to carry. The muzzle was the preferred weapon when he first began an battle.

BOMBS

Black Powder

Black powder is made up consisting of charcoal, sulfur as well as potassium in nitrate (saltpeter). Both charcoal and sulfur are fuels, while the saltpeter functions as an oxygenizer. Due to its fire-producing properties black powder is able to produce an enormous quantity of heat and gas volume in a short time. It is the reason why it is not used only to propel firearms but also as an explosive.

The pirates who used black powder bombs, they produced explosives at subsonic speed. This was considered to be a weak explosive, but it isn't nearly comparable to the explosions that are used in today's. Powder bombs made of black were great to divert attention or removing the weight of a door. The bombs did not have enough force to break open rocks or stone fortifications. This made their use only limited.

Grenados

Grenados were an early, explosive with black powder that was popular among pirates. The term grenado comes by the French word meaning pomegranate. which is the fruit that the bomb was akin to. The grenade is typically composed of a hollow iron ball, however a hollow clay balls, an empty tin ball, or a bottles could be utilized. The ball can range between about the size of a tiny orange up to the size the grapefruit of a huge size. The size of a fist was the most efficient for throwing.

The iron ball was cast with usually one opening that is filled with gunpowder shrapnel, and shot. Shrapnel found in grenados might be nails, broken glass or even scrap iron. A single hole is then closed with a fuse. A typical fuse consisted of strings or cotton that could ignite, but not enough fast for pirates to remove the flame before it went out. Another popular fuse in the era was the black match. The kind of simple fuse was made of strings of cotton that had been coated by a slurry of black powder. If the match of black is contained in a paper tube, it's called a rapid match. Its fire burns more rapidly and can reach a distance of several feet at a time.

The fuse ignited, and the grenade directed towards the area of the target. This was particularly effective when it was in a protected area where the blast would guide the blast. It was a good sound to shock the occupants. They probably cause more injury from burned and shrapnel than were able to cause fatalities. Although not as effective as modern grenades pirate's grenados were quite loud and deadly under the right circumstances.

Chapter 19: Stinkpots

In naval operations, the stinkpot served as an explosive device, which contained an suffocating agent in addition. The most common type of ceramic or similar earthenware vessel was utilized to create the shell for the device. After that, it was packed with sulfur, cotton gunpowder or any other substance which could be harmful if the fire was lit. Other ingredients utilized included plant gums decayed meats, fish that was rotten as well as feces.

The stinkpot is lit as a grenade, and dropped by hand or shot by catapult on vessels of the enemy. Another method for delivery would be rolling it below the decks along borders to disperse crew members who were shackled. When the fire was ignited, it resulted in the creation of a basic version that was a tear gas. The gas would trigger burning of the nose, eyes and throat. It also caused vomiting.

Close to the enemy, the smell would overwhelm and these fumes could blind enemies. The burning gasses could kill any person who tries to stay the air. In the event that crew members were denied oxygen inside the tight confines and the insufficient ventilation lower decks of the vessel could have proved fatal and efficient. It could be regarded as one of the first forms of chemical warfare.

Fire Bombs

A fire bomb is an incendiary weapon that was specifically designed to set off fires. It can be extremely useful in combating wooden vessels. Of course, the trick was to avoid burning the whole ship until its load could be removed from the vessel. Rigging and sails were the preferred target in this instance. But fire bombs can damage both sides the attacker as well as the target when used in a manner that isn't properly.

SPECIALIZED WEAPONS

Caltrop (Crow's Foot)

Caltrops are often described by the name of the crow's-foot, because of its form was usually made of scrap metal that was shaped into a form with the protruding four points. Its roots can be traced through the ages when Romans employed them as a foil to protect war-chariots. The benefit of having Four Points was, when dropped, they would have at the very least one point pointing up. The sailors used to walk in barefoot, so throwing caltrop on the deck could cause damage including injury to the crew members of a vessel that was attacked. It could also serve to defend. If they were thrown in the direction of boarders, they could delay enemy sailors and cause chaos in the water.

It is used to defend wheels-driven vehicles. The caltrop has been called many variations of names throughout the years, including and not just the galtrop, caltrop trap galthrap, calthrop, and as mentioned previously, the Crow's Foot.

Grappling Hook

A grappling hook is a piece of equipment equipped with several hooks (typically three) also known as claws or flukes and were secured to an underlying shaft. The shaft featured an eye on its base of which a rope fixed. They were useful because when they were they were thrown, at most one, they would have an opening.

The grappling hook could be dropped by pirates on the bow or rigging on the enemy vessel, so that the vessel could be dragged towards the bow to board. This maneuver required the use of a grappling hook was crucial to the whole operation. If properly used, it can be utilized, with plenty of muscles in order to drag the adversary ship closer to a pirate ship so in order for the crew to jump or step from their own gunwale and onto the deck of the enemy.

A different method for boarding was pirates using a dory gig, or rowboat. The boat with a smaller size can be positioned alongside the vessel that was in conflict, when the conditions permitted grappling hooks also proved vital as they were employed to attach the gunwales of the enemy. Pirates were able to take off with the attached ropes.

Grappling hooks remain being used and are typically handed thrown. However, the use of compressed air, firearm mounted as well as crossbow mounted hooks are readily available.

Pirate Flag

The flag of the pirate was numerous times the first offensive line. The flag was used to scare those who were enemies of the pirates to surrender without a fighting.

The flag signalled to the ship they were aiming at that the pirates were outlaws who were not legally bound to the normal norms of engagement in naval warfare. The merchant captain may have his entire crew killed while pirates were likely to fight until the end of time as the penalty for piracy would be hanging. The sight of a flag of the pirates would prompt vessels to fly a white flag to negotiate terms.

The black flag was the most frequently used flag of pirates. A Jolly Roger was the most popular. Jolly Roger is the most famous and popular flag used in the Golden Age of Piracy. A lot of famous people utilized this Jolly Roger; the traditional skull, with two tibias crossing with an X-shape, such as Captains "Black Sam" Bellamy, John Taylor and Edward England.

www.ingramcontent.com/pod-product-compliance
Lightning Source LLC
Chambersburg PA
CBHW071338120626
46546CB00002B/613